The
Professor's
Daughter

JOANN SFAR & EMMANUEL GUIBERT

The Professor's Daughter

TRANSLATED BY ALEXIS SIEGEL

:01

First Second
NEW YORK & LONDON

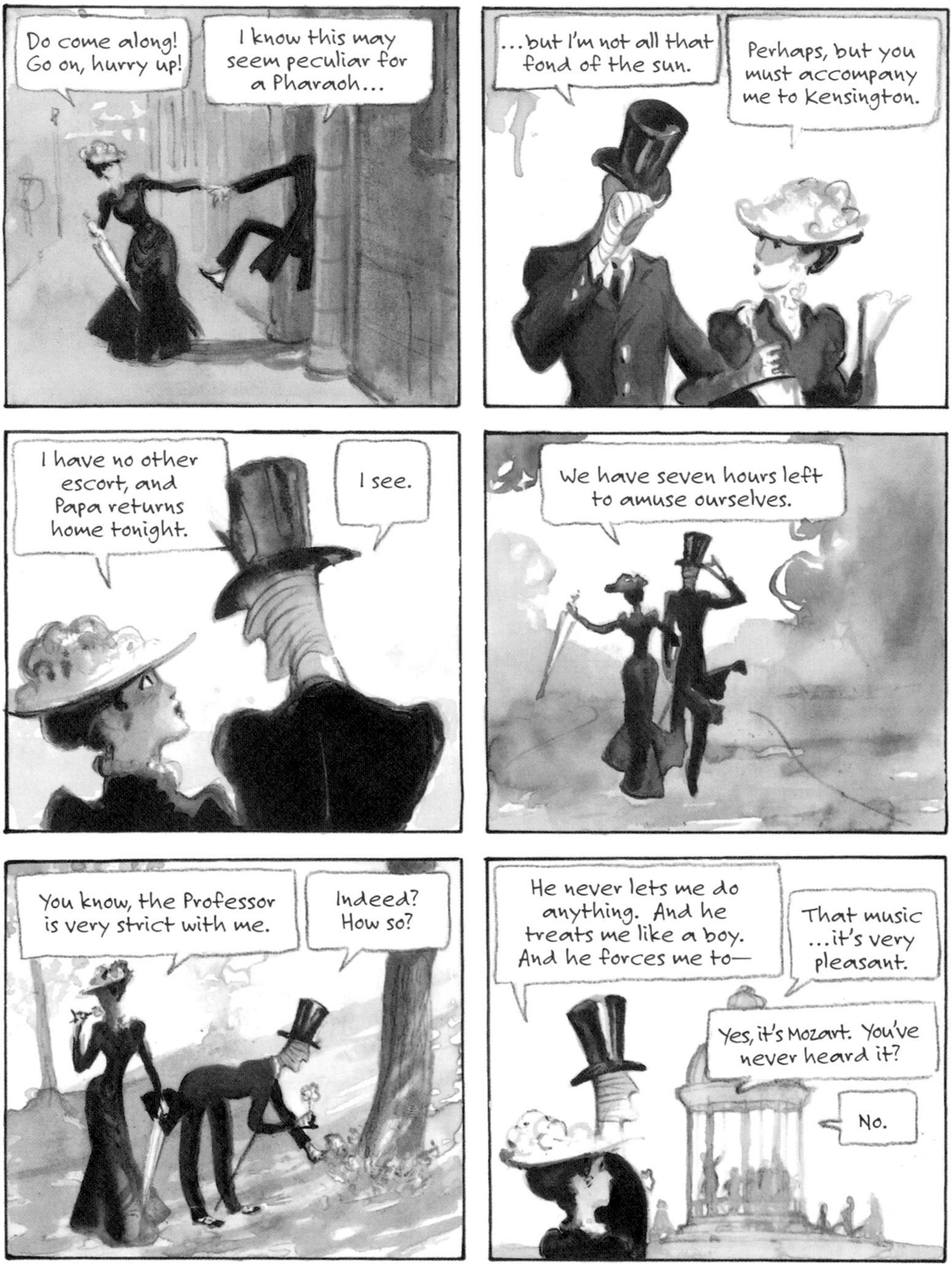
Do come along! Go on, hurry up!
I know this may seem peculiar for a Pharaoh...
...but I'm not all that fond of the sun.
Perhaps, but you must accompany me to Kensington.
I have no other escort, and Papa returns home tonight.
I see.
We have seven hours left to amuse ourselves.
You know, the Professor is very strict with me.
Indeed? How so?
He never lets me do anything. And he treats me like a boy. And he forces me to—
That music ...it's very pleasant.
Yes, it's Mozart. You've never heard it?
No.

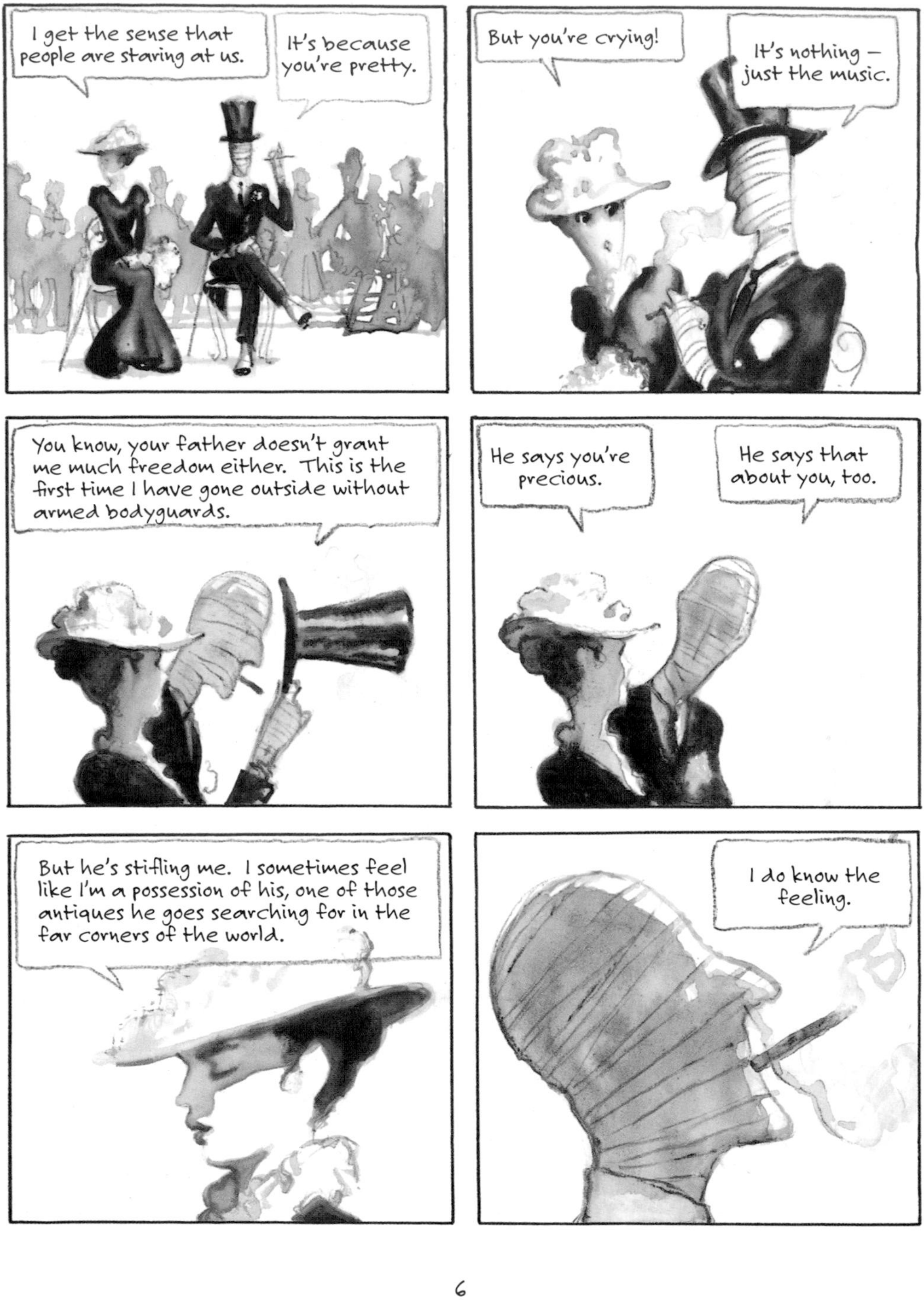
I get the sense that people are staring at us.
It's because you're pretty.
But you're crying!
It's nothing — just the music.
You know, your father doesn't grant me much freedom either. This is the first time I have gone outside without armed bodyguards.
He says you're precious.
He says that about you, too.
But he's stifling me. I sometimes feel like I'm a possession of his, one of those antiques he goes searching for in the far corners of the world.
I do know the feeling.

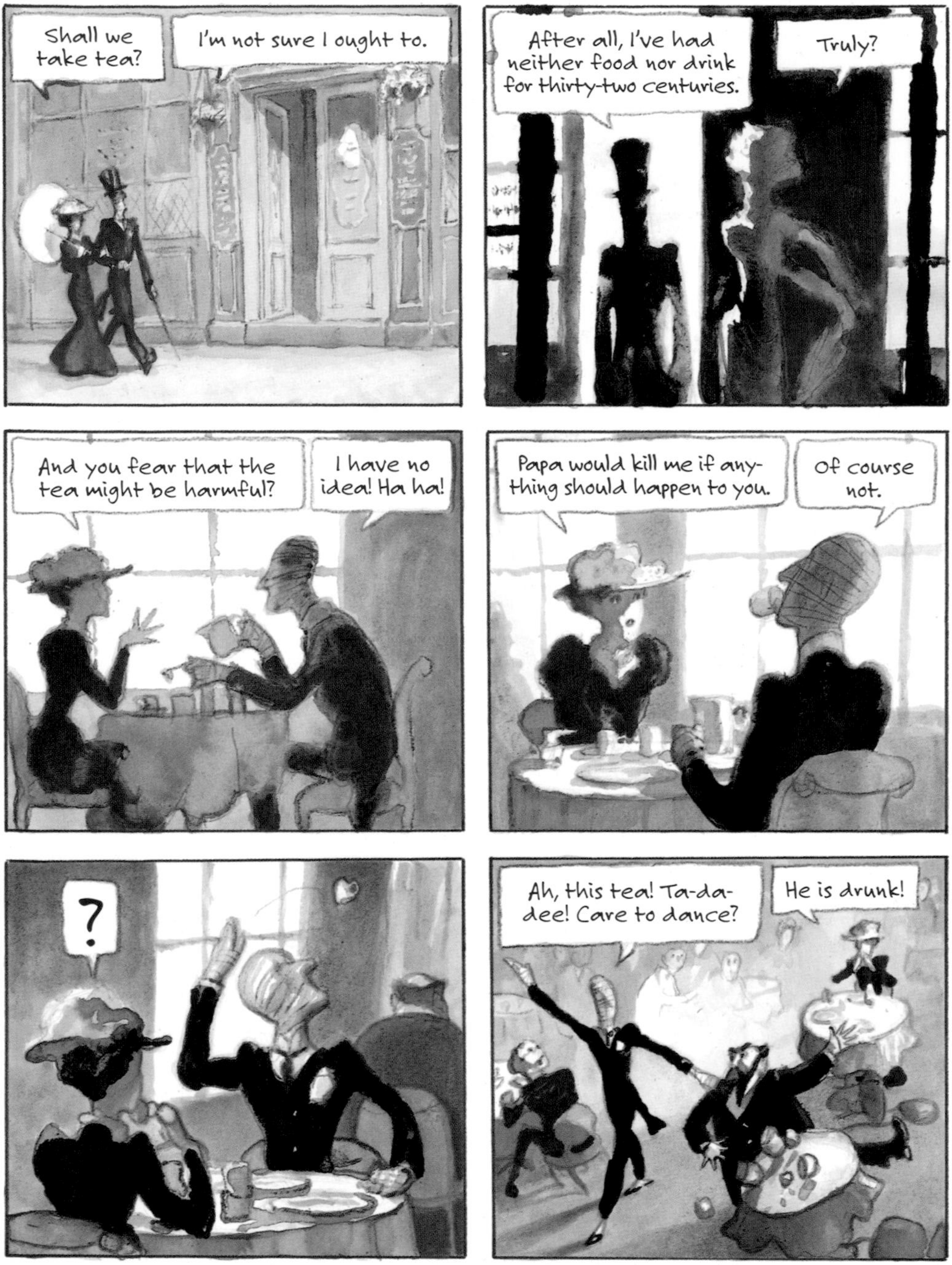
Shall we take tea?
I'm not sure I ought to.
After all, I've had neither food nor drink for thirty-two centuries.
Truly?
And you fear that the tea might be harmful?
I have no idea! Ha ha!
Papa would kill me if anything should happen to you.
Of course not.
?
Ah, this tea! Ta-da-dee! Care to dance?
He is drunk!

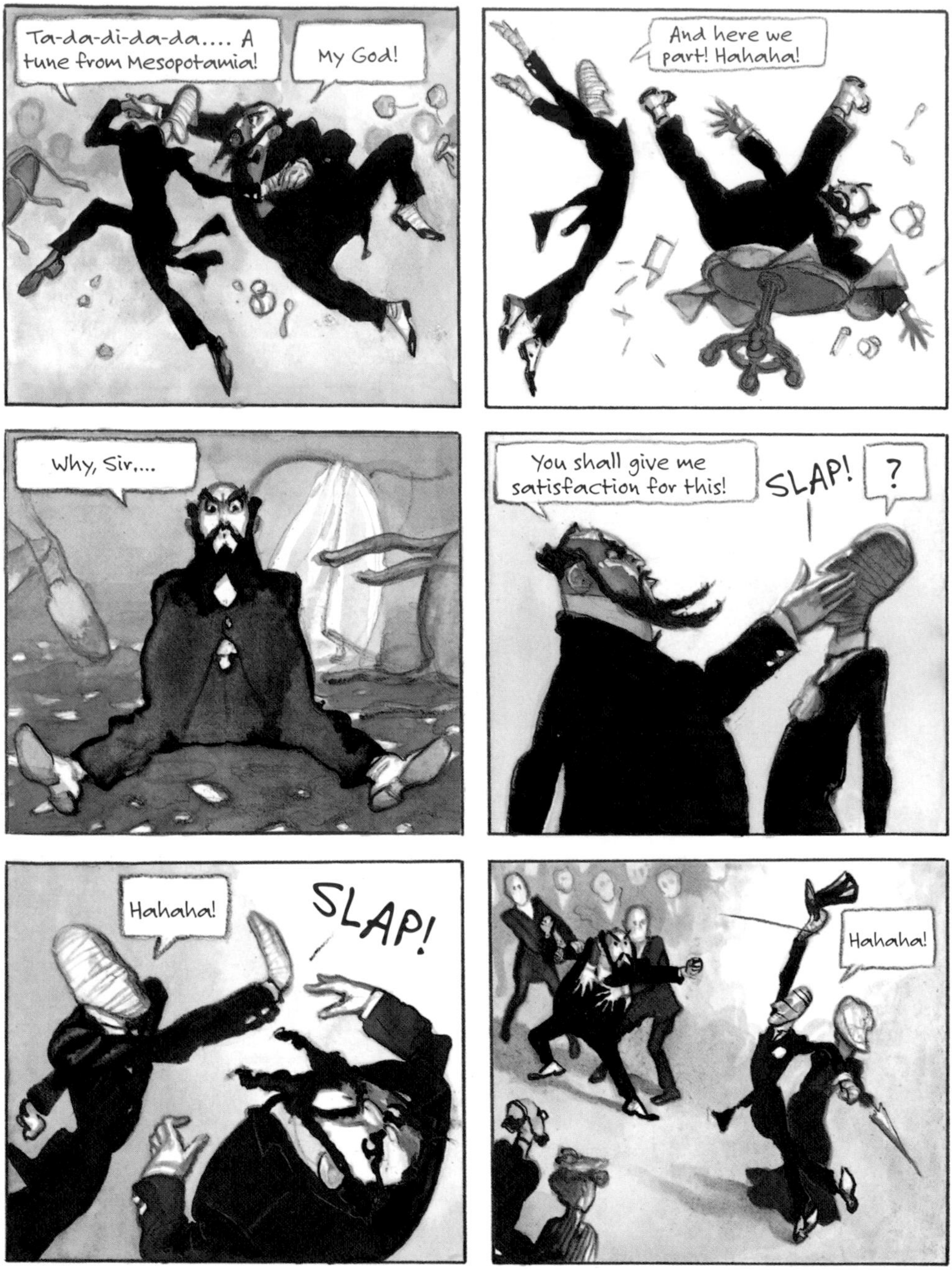
Ta-da-di-da-da.... A tune from Mesopotamia!
My God!
And here we part! Hahaha!
Why, Sir,...
You shall give me satisfaction for this!
SLAP!
?
Hahaha!
SLAP!
Hahaha!

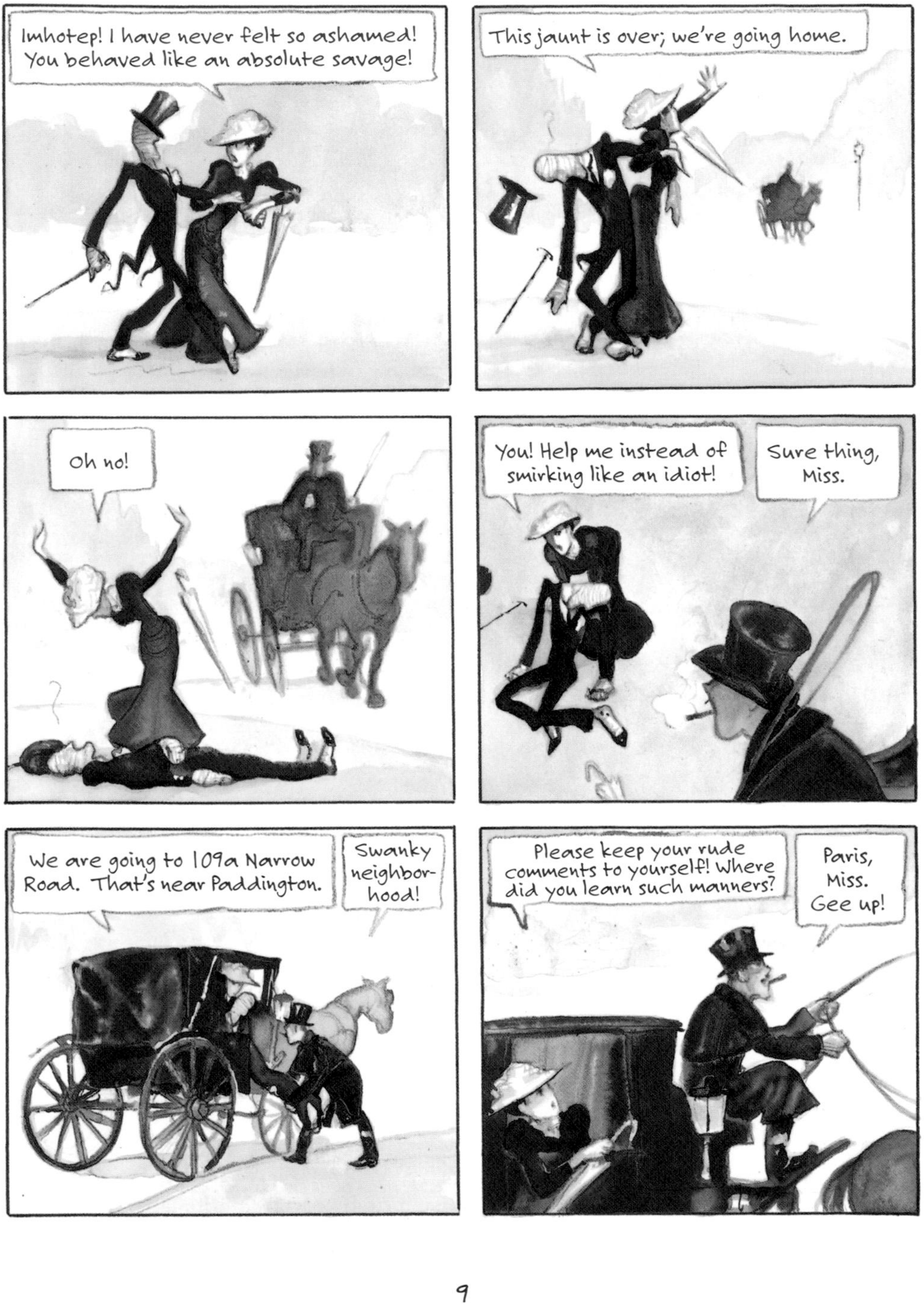
Imhotep! I have never felt so ashamed! You behaved like an absolute savage!
This jaunt is over; we're going home.
Oh no!
You! Help me instead of smirking like an idiot!
Sure thing, Miss.
We are going to 109a Narrow Road. That's near Paddington.
Swanky neighbor-hood!
Please keep your rude comments to yourself! Where did you learn such manners?
Paris, Miss. Gee up!

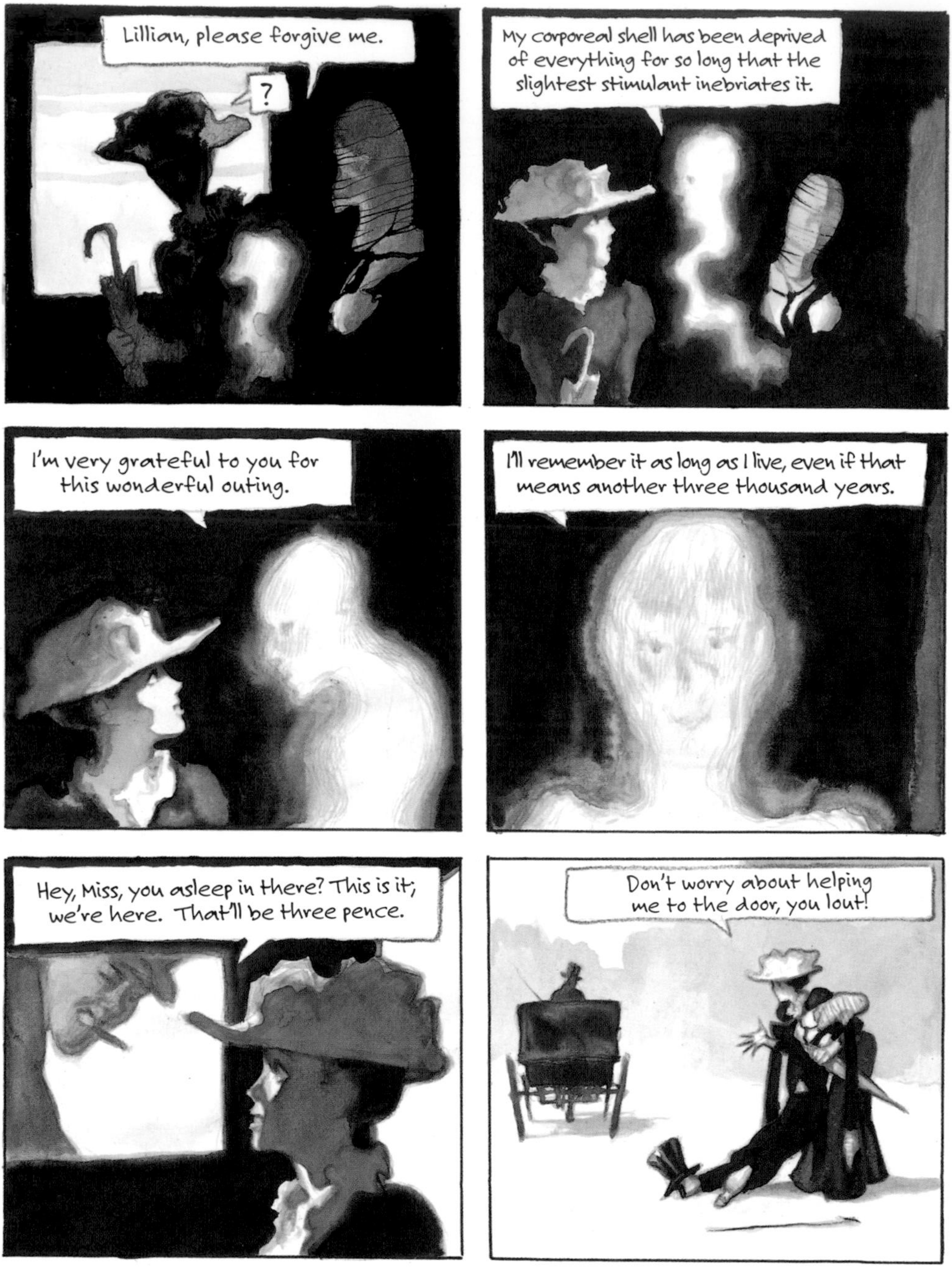
Lillian, please forgive me.
?
My corporeal shell has been deprived of everything for so long that the slightest stimulant inebriates it.
I'm very grateful to you for this wonderful outing.
I'll remember it as long as I live, even if that means another three thousand years.
Hey, Miss, you asleep in there? This is it; we're here. That'll be three pence.
Don't worry about helping me to the door, you lout!

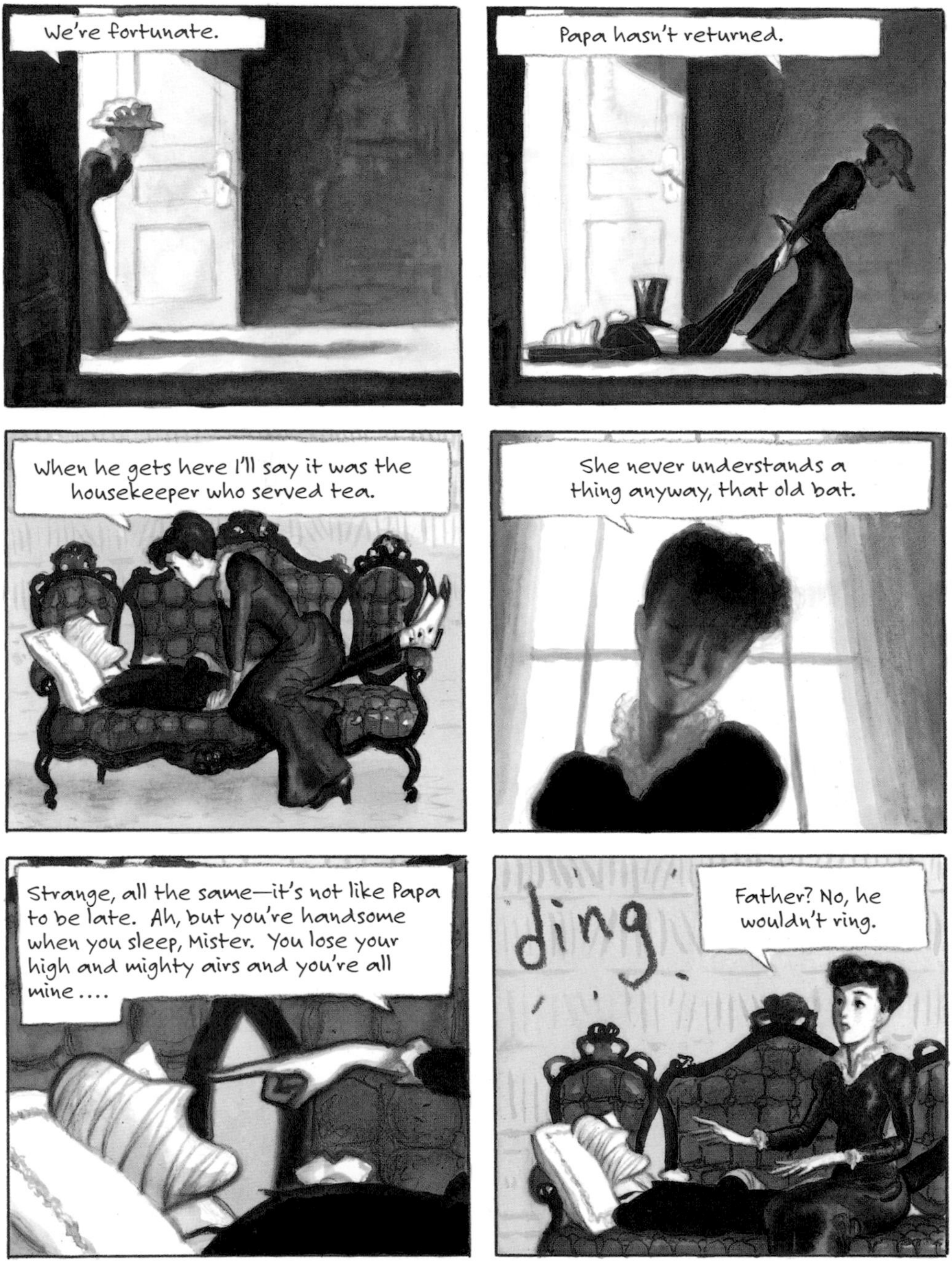
We're fortunate.
Papa hasn't returned.
When he gets here I'll say it was the housekeeper who served tea.
She never understands a thing anyway, that old bat.
Strange, all the same—it's not like Papa to be late. Ah, but you're handsome when you sleep, Mister. You lose your high and mighty airs and you're all mine....
ding
Father? No, he wouldn't ring.

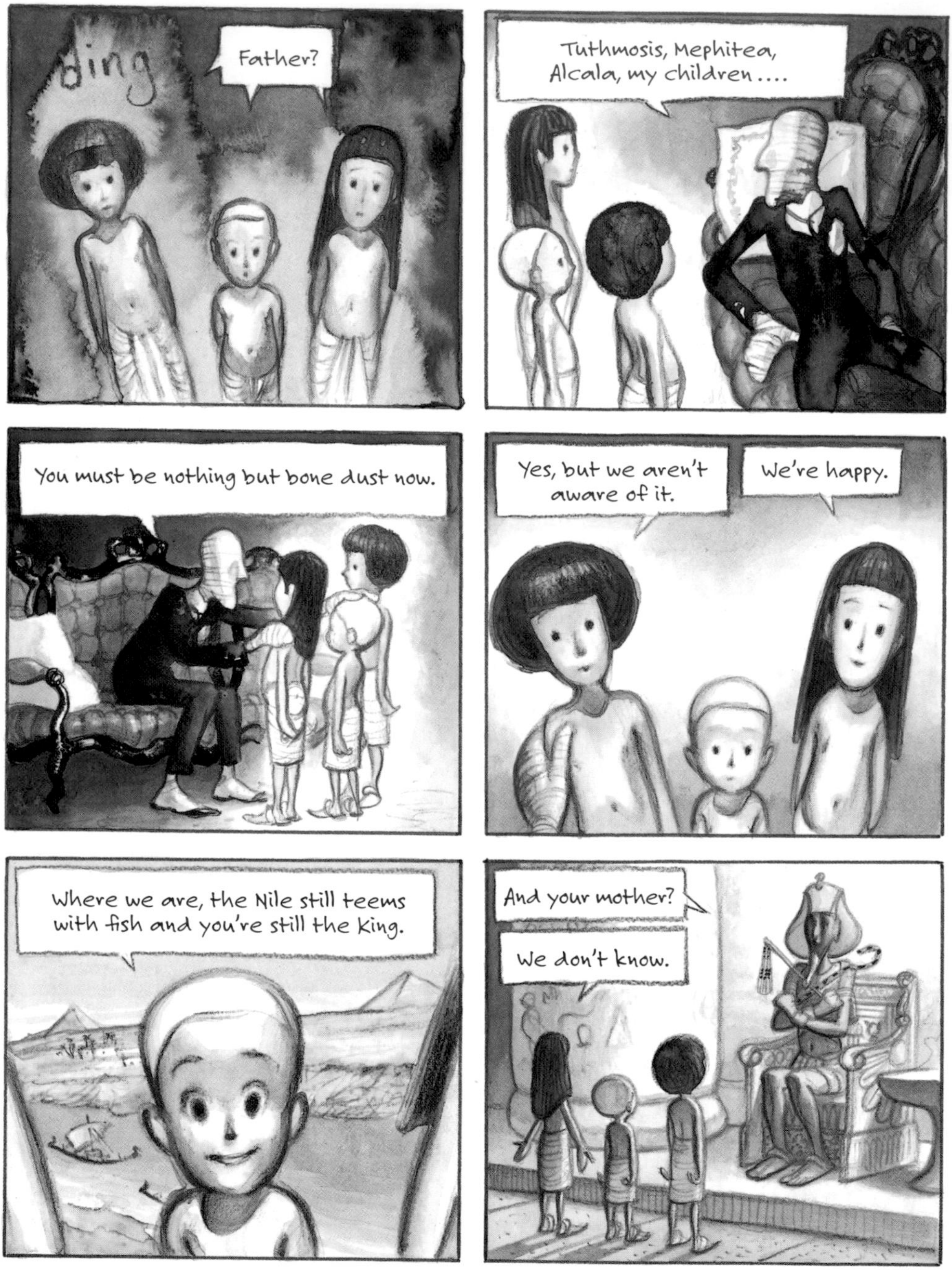
ding
Father?
Tuthmosis, Mephitea, Alcala, my children....
You must be nothing but bone dust now.
Yes, but we aren't aware of it.
We're happy.
Where we are, the Nile still teems with fish and you're still the King.
And your mother?
We don't know.

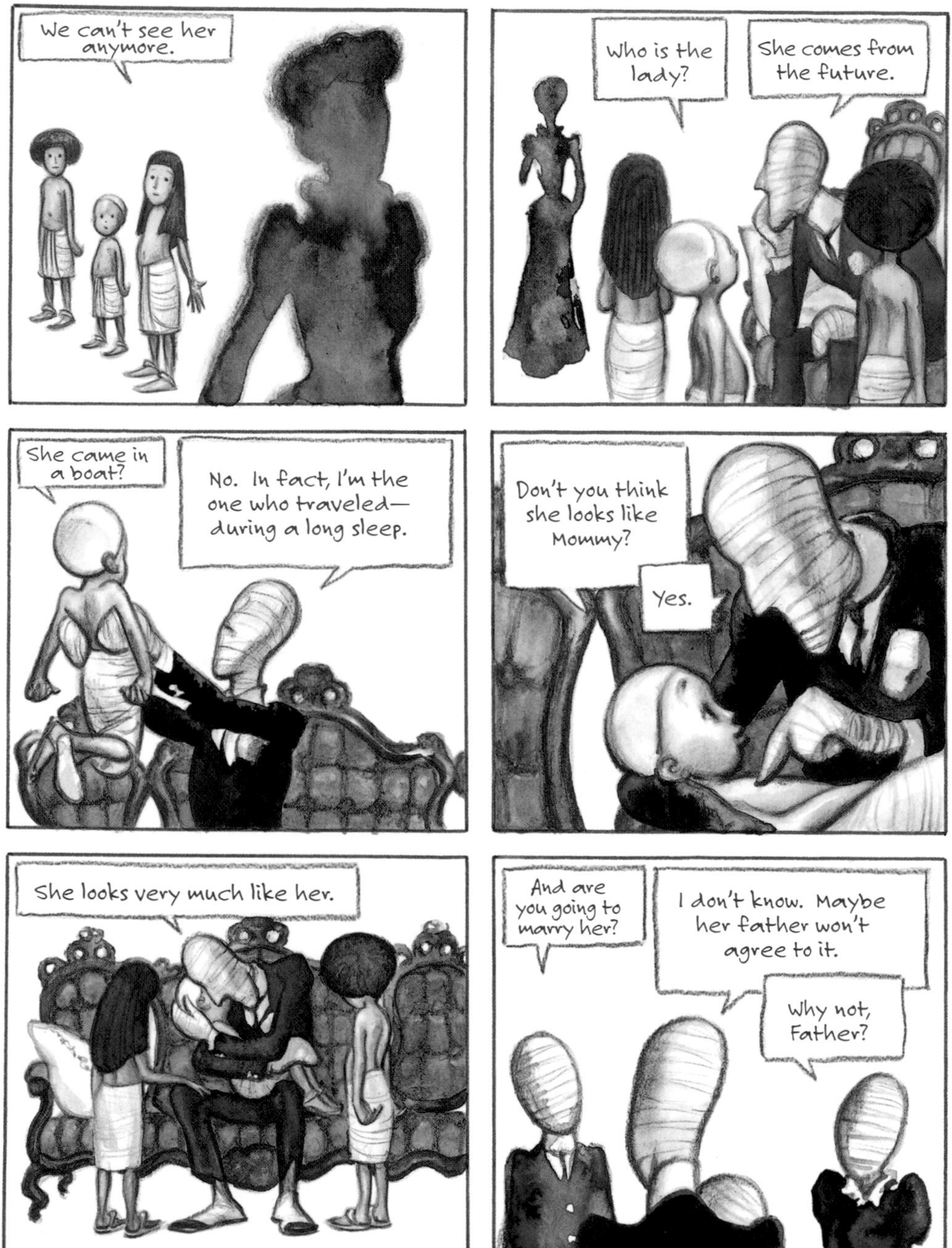
We can't see her anymore.
Who is the lady?
She comes from the future.
She came in a boat?
No. In fact, I'm the one who traveled— during a long sleep.
Don't you think she looks like Mommy?
Yes.
She looks very much like her.
And are you going to marry her?
I don't know. Maybe her father won't agree to it.
Why not, Father?

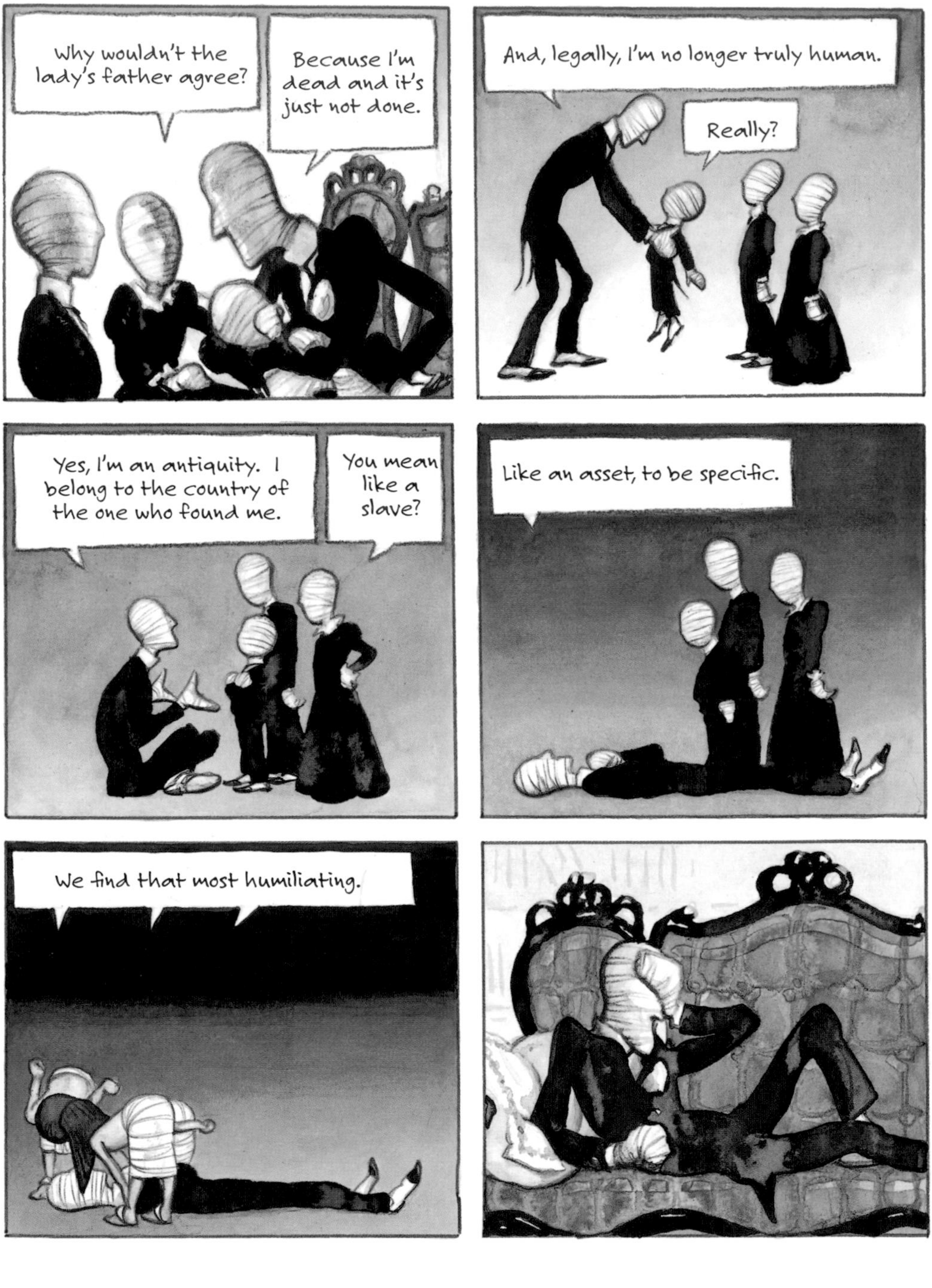
Why wouldn't the lady's father agree?
Because I'm dead and it's just not done.
And, legally, I'm no longer truly human.
Really?
Yes, I'm an antiquity. I belong to the country of the one who found me.
You mean like a slave?
Like an asset, to be specific.
We find that most humiliating.

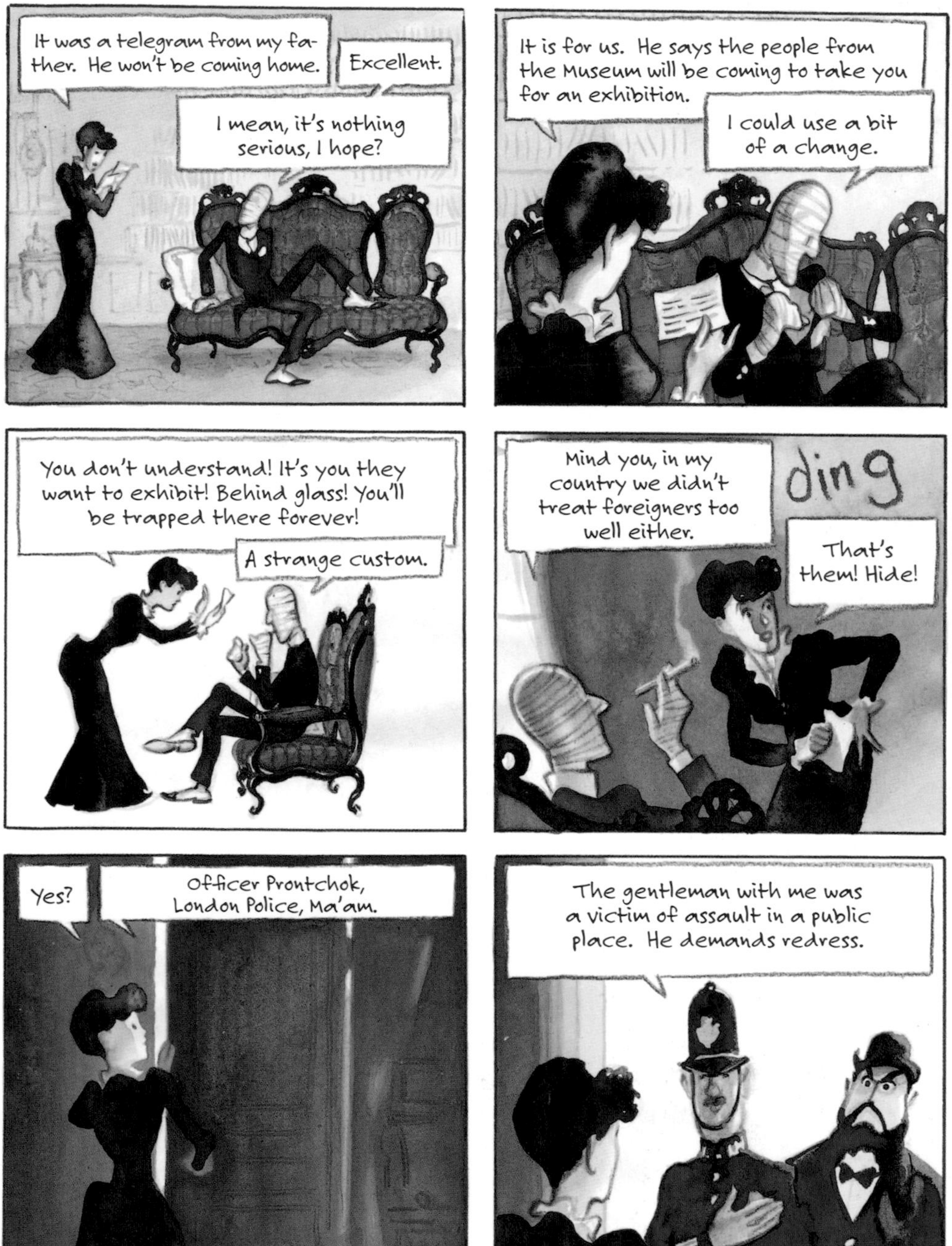
It was a telegram from my father. He won't be coming home.
Excellent.
I mean, it's nothing serious, I hope?
It is for us. He says the people from the Museum will be coming to take you for an exhibition.
I could use a bit of a change.
You don't understand! It's you they want to exhibit! Behind glass! You'll be trapped there forever!
A strange custom.
Mind you, in my country we didn't treat foreigners too well either.
ding
That's them! Hide!
Yes?
Officer Prontchok, London Police, Ma'am.
The gentleman with me was a victim of assault in a public place. He demands redress.

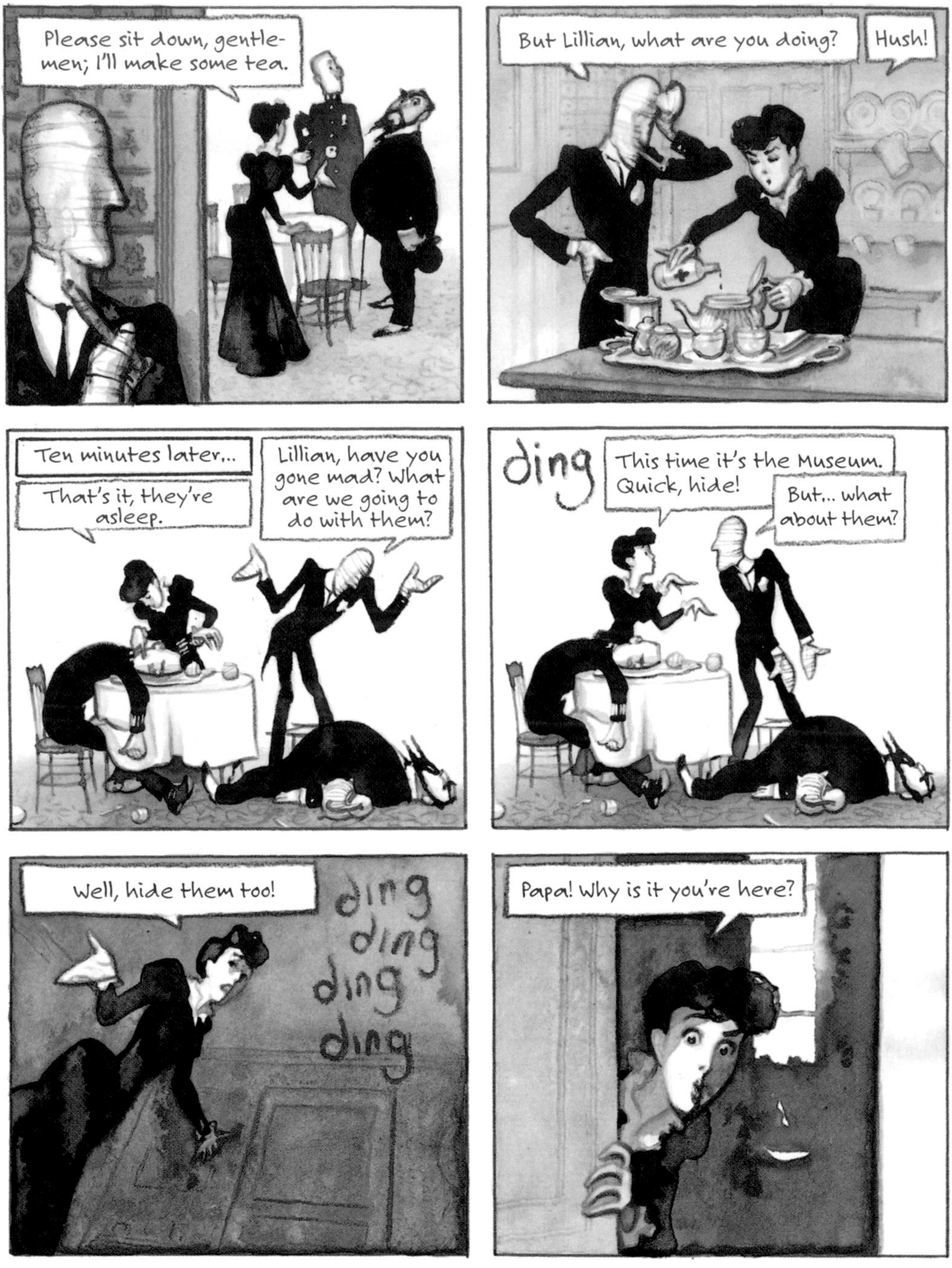
Please sit down, gentlemen; I'll make some tea.
But Lillian, what are you doing?
Hush!
Ten minutes later...
That's it, they're asleep.
Lillian, have you gone mad? What are we going to do with them?
ding
This time it's the Museum. Quick, hide!
But... what about them?
Well, hide them too!
ding ding ding ding
Papa! Why is it you're here?

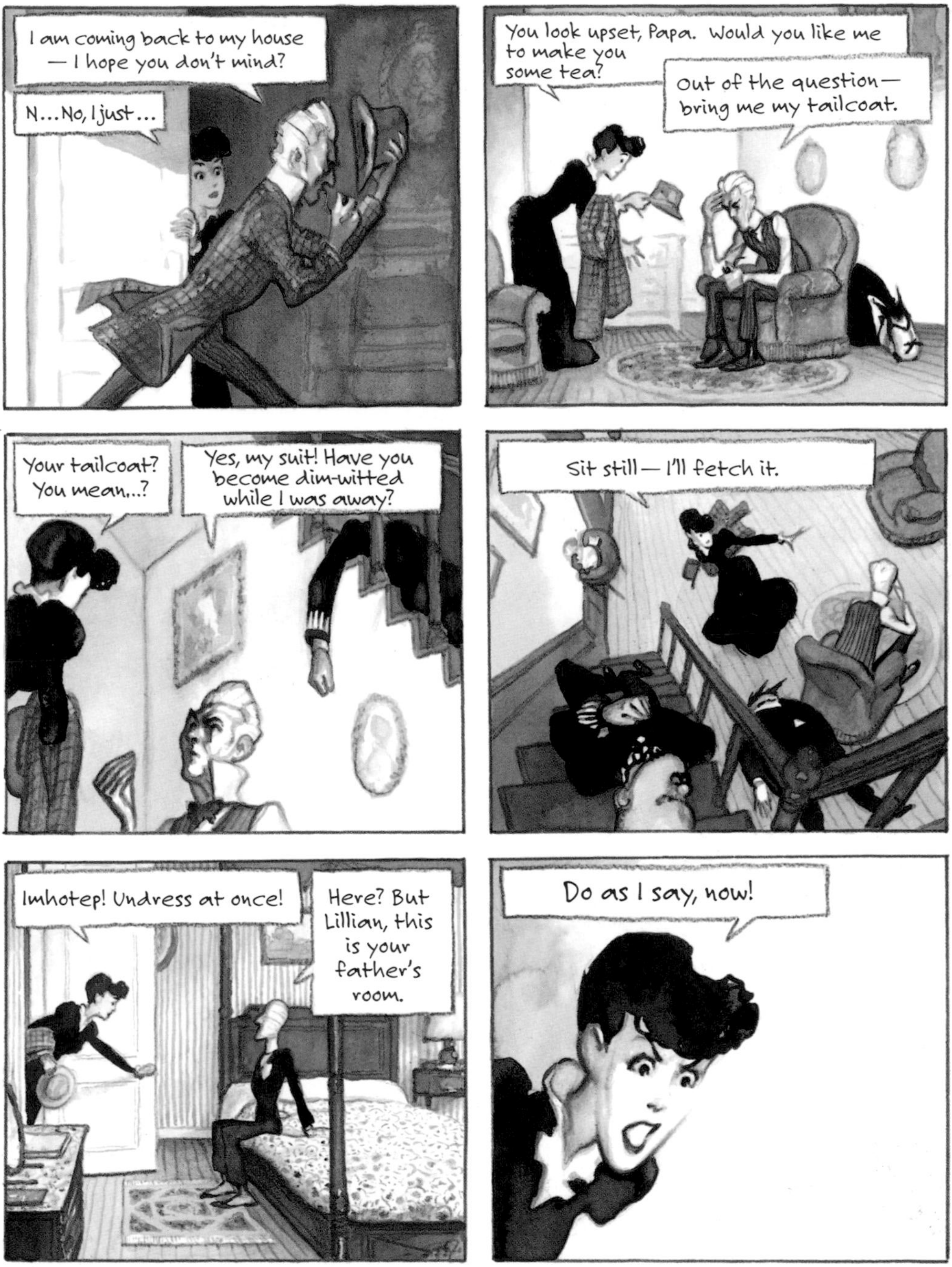
I am coming back to my house — I hope you don't mind?
N... No, I just...
You look upset, Papa. Would you like me to make you some tea?
Out of the question— bring me my tailcoat.
Your tailcoat? You mean...?
Yes, my suit! Have you become dim-witted while I was away?
Sit still— I'll fetch it.
Imhotep! Undress at once!
Here? But Lillian, this is your father's room.
Do as I say, now!

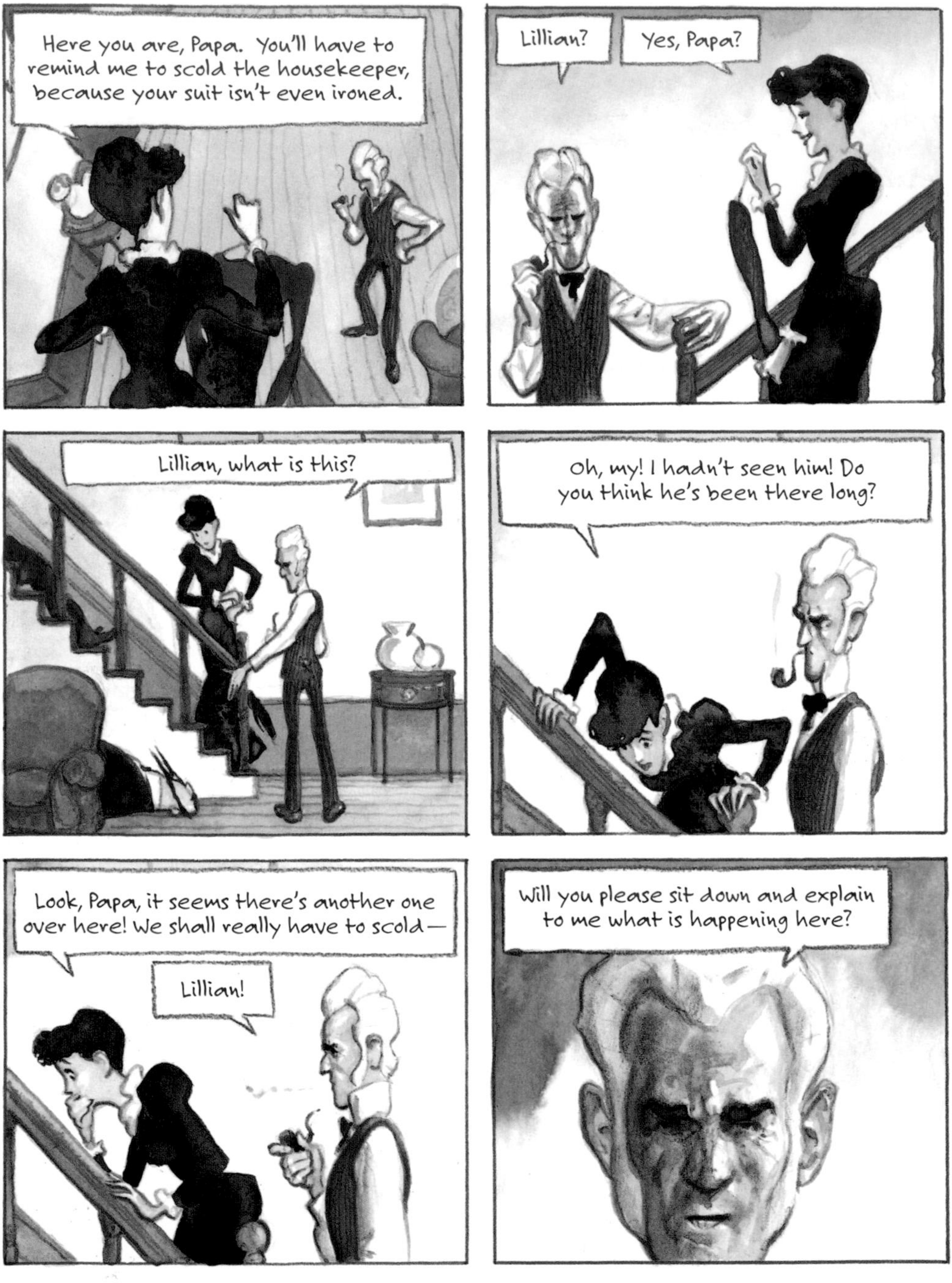
Here you are, Papa. You'll have to remind me to scold the housekeeper, because your suit isn't even ironed.
Lillian?
Yes, Papa?
Lillian, what is this?
Oh, my! I hadn't seen him! Do you think he's been there long?
Look, Papa, it seems there's another one over here! We shall really have to scold—
Lillian!
Will you please sit down and explain to me what is happening here?

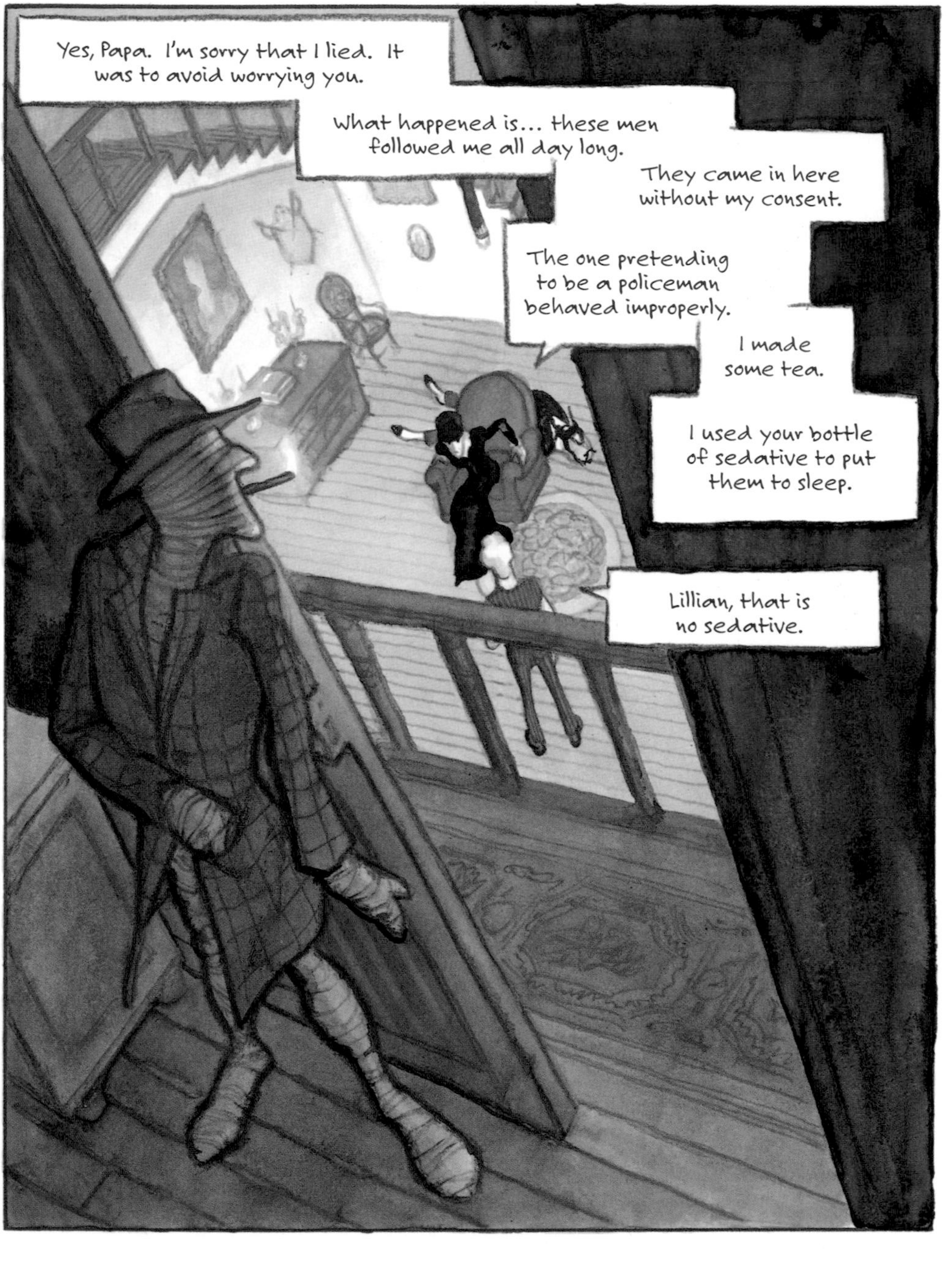

Yes, Papa. I'm sorry that I lied. It was to avoid worrying you.
What happened is... these men followed me all day long.
They came in here without my consent.
The one pretending to be a policeman behaved improperly.
I made some tea.
I used your bottle of sedative to put them to sleep.
Lillian, that is no sedative.

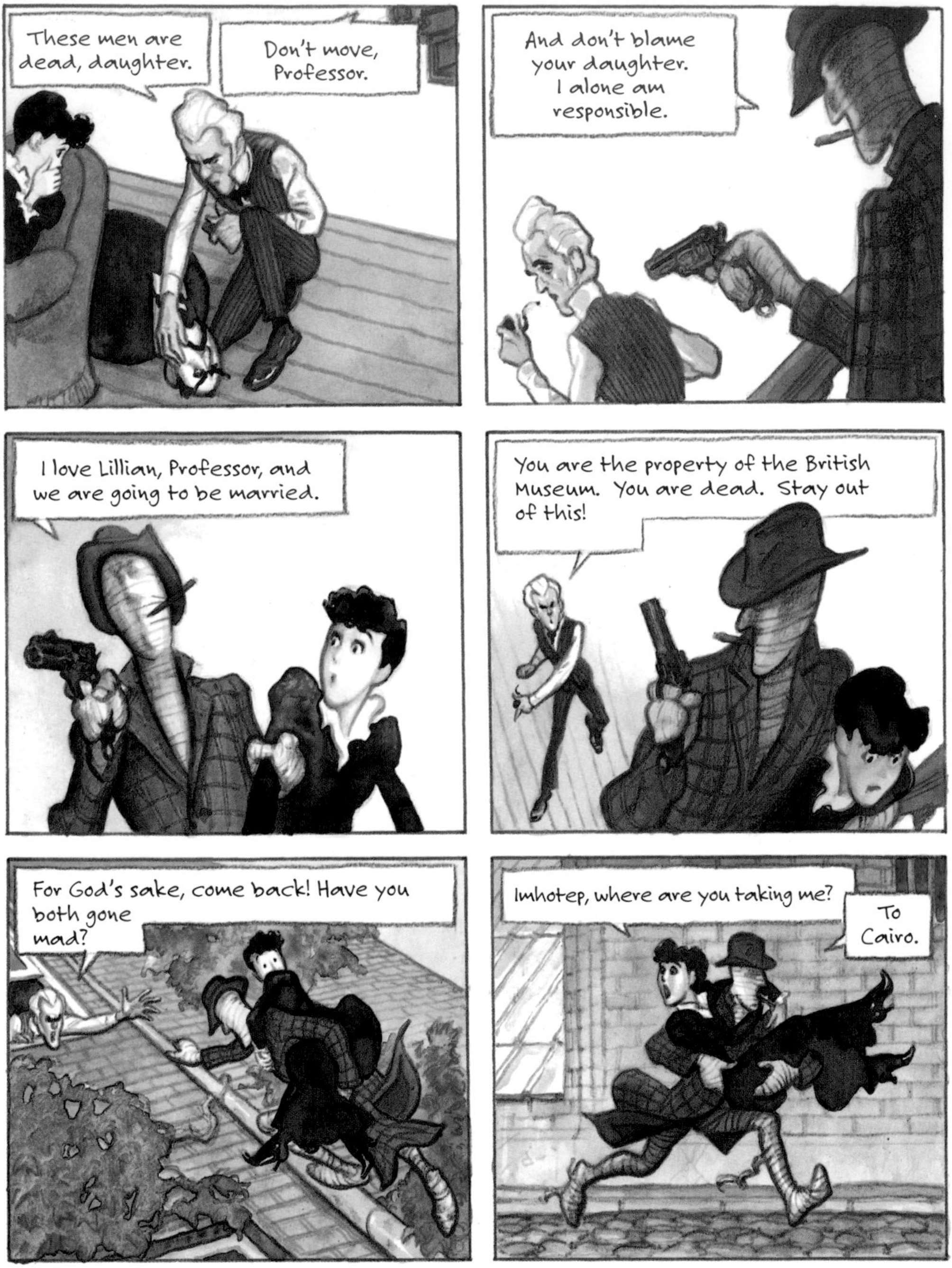
These men are dead, daughter.
Don't move, Professor.
And don't blame your daughter. I alone am responsible.
I love Lillian, Professor, and we are going to be married.
You are the property of the British Museum. You are dead. Stay out of this!
For God's sake, come back! Have you both gone mad?
Imhotep, where are you taking me?
To Cairo.

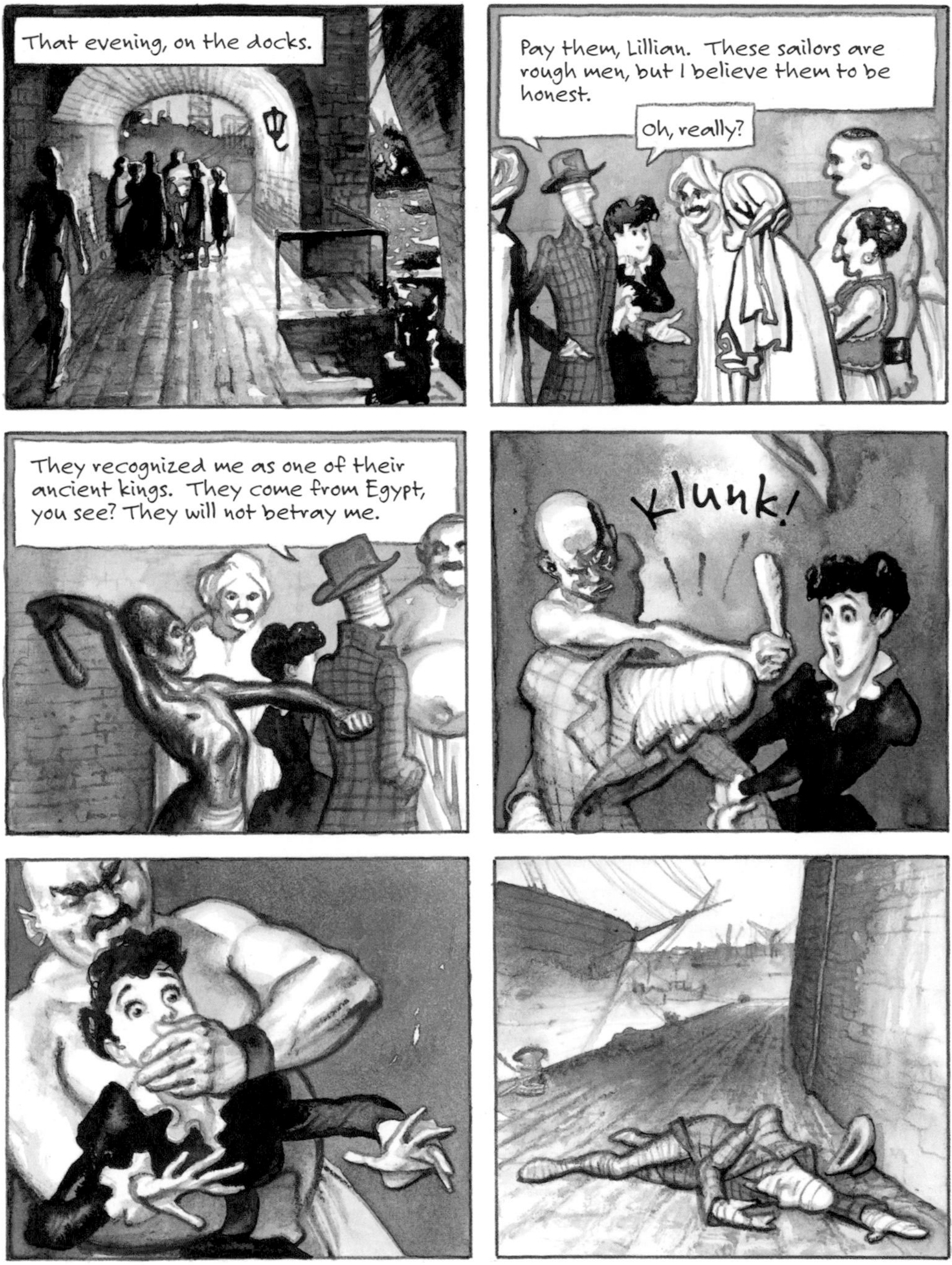
That evening, on the docks.
Pay them, Lillian. These sailors are rough men, but I believe them to be honest.
Oh, really?
They recognized me as one of their ancient kings. They come from Egypt, you see? They will not betray me.
Klunk!

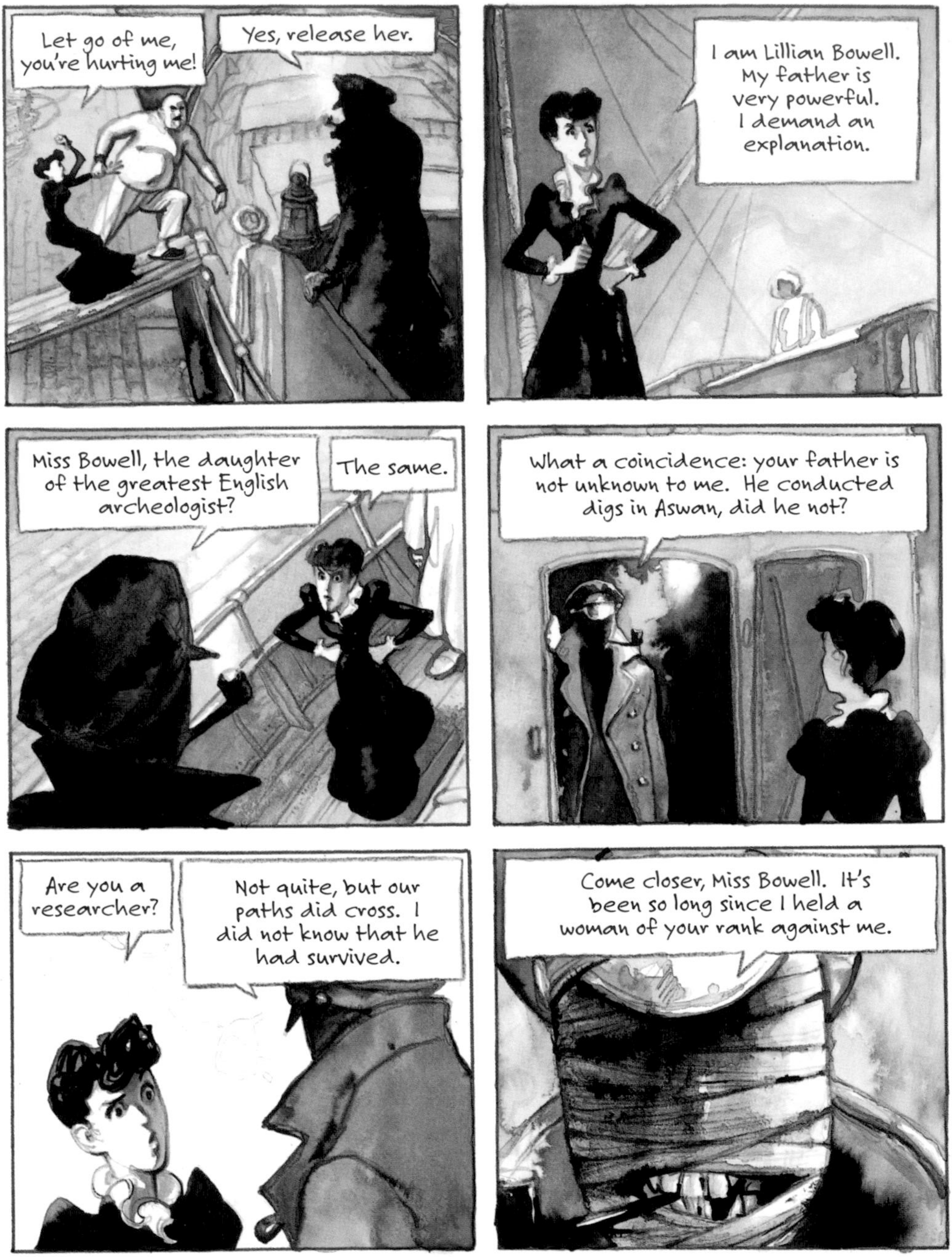
Let go of me, you're hurting me!
Yes, release her.
I am Lillian Bowell. My father is very powerful. I demand an explanation.
Miss Bowell, the daughter of the greatest English archeologist?
The same.
What a coincidence: your father is not unknown to me. He conducted digs in Aswan, did he not?
Are you a researcher?
Not quite, but our paths did cross. I did not know that he had survived.
Come closer, Miss Bowell. It's been so long since I held a woman of your rank against me.

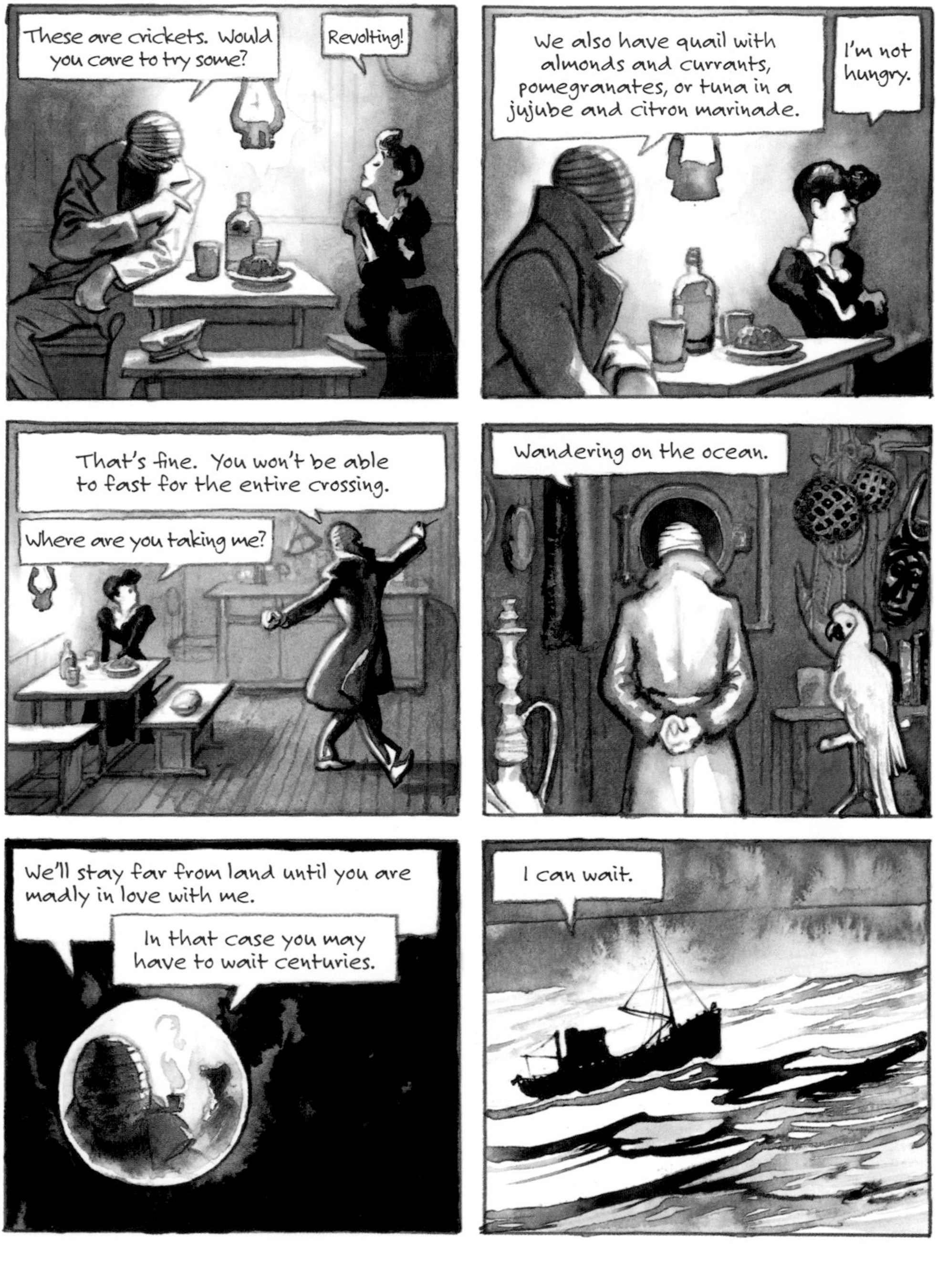
These are crickets. Would you care to try some?
Revolting!
We also have quail with almonds and currants, pomegranates, or tuna in a jujube and citron marinade.
I'm not hungry.
That's fine. You won't be able to fast for the entire crossing.
Where are you taking me?
Wandering on the ocean.
We'll stay far from land until you are madly in love with me.
In that case you may have to wait centuries.
I can wait.

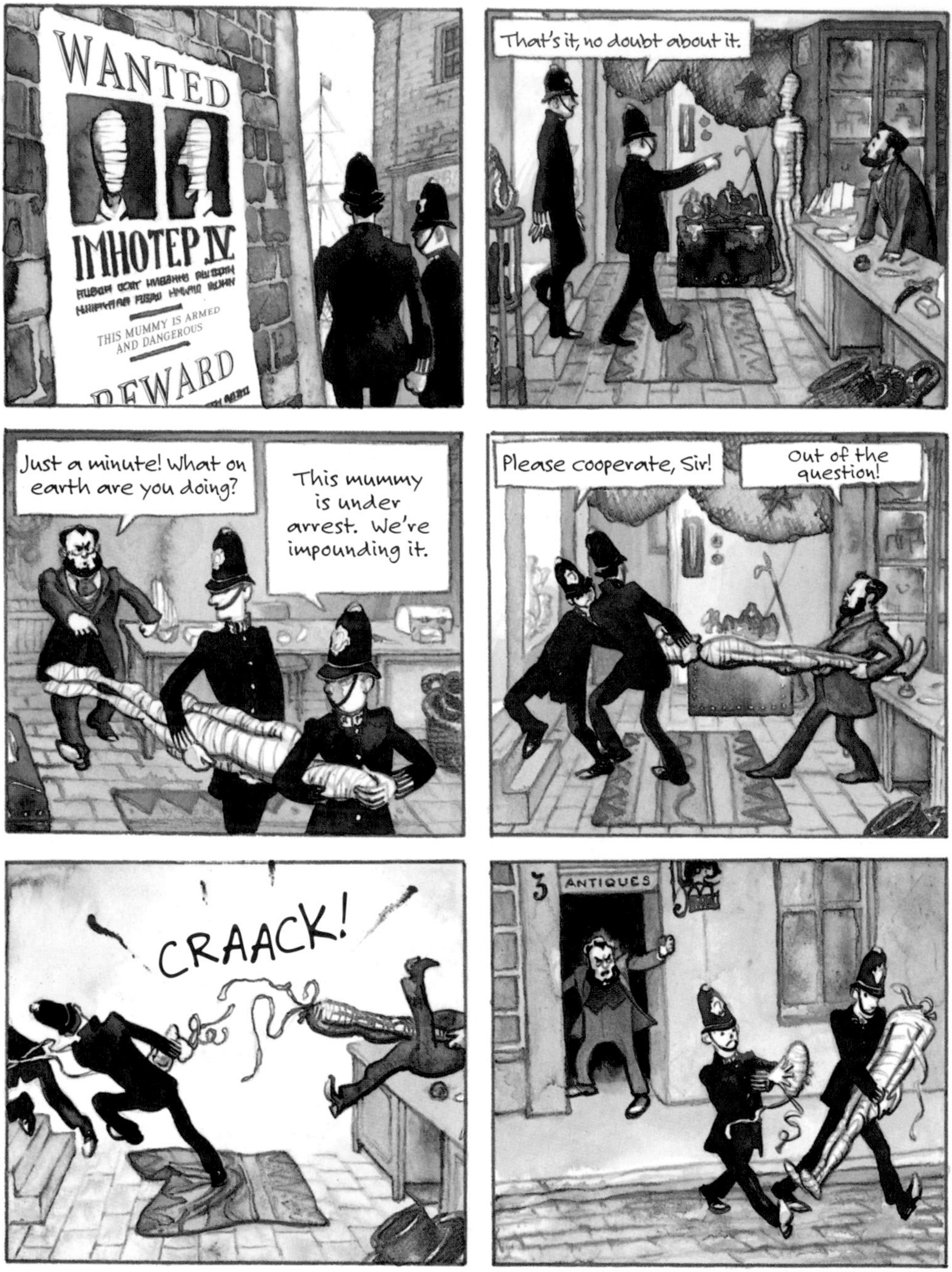
WANTED
IMHOTEP IV
THIS MUMMY IS ARMED AND DANGEROUS
REWARD
That's it, no doubt about it.
Just a minute! What on earth are you doing?
This mummy is under arrest. We're impounding it.
Please cooperate, Sir!
Out of the question!
CRAACK!
3
ANTIQUES

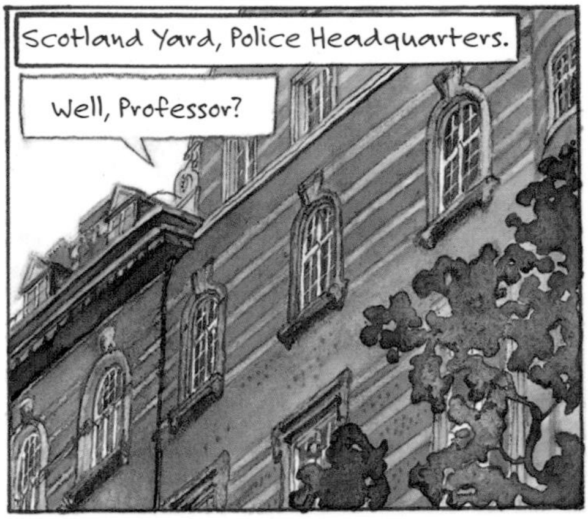
Scotland Yard, Police Headquarters.
Well, Professor?

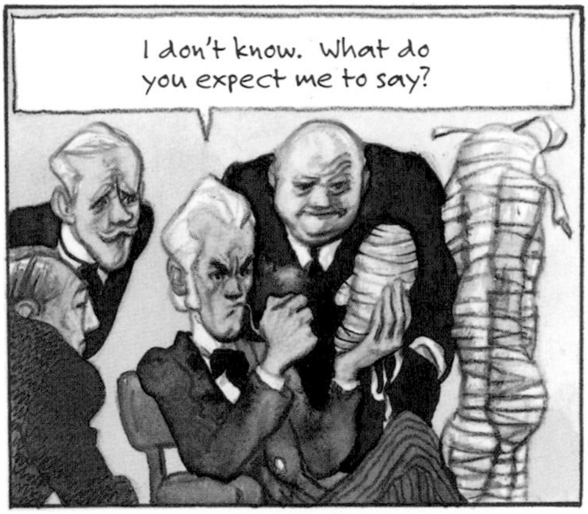
I don't know. What do you expect me to say?

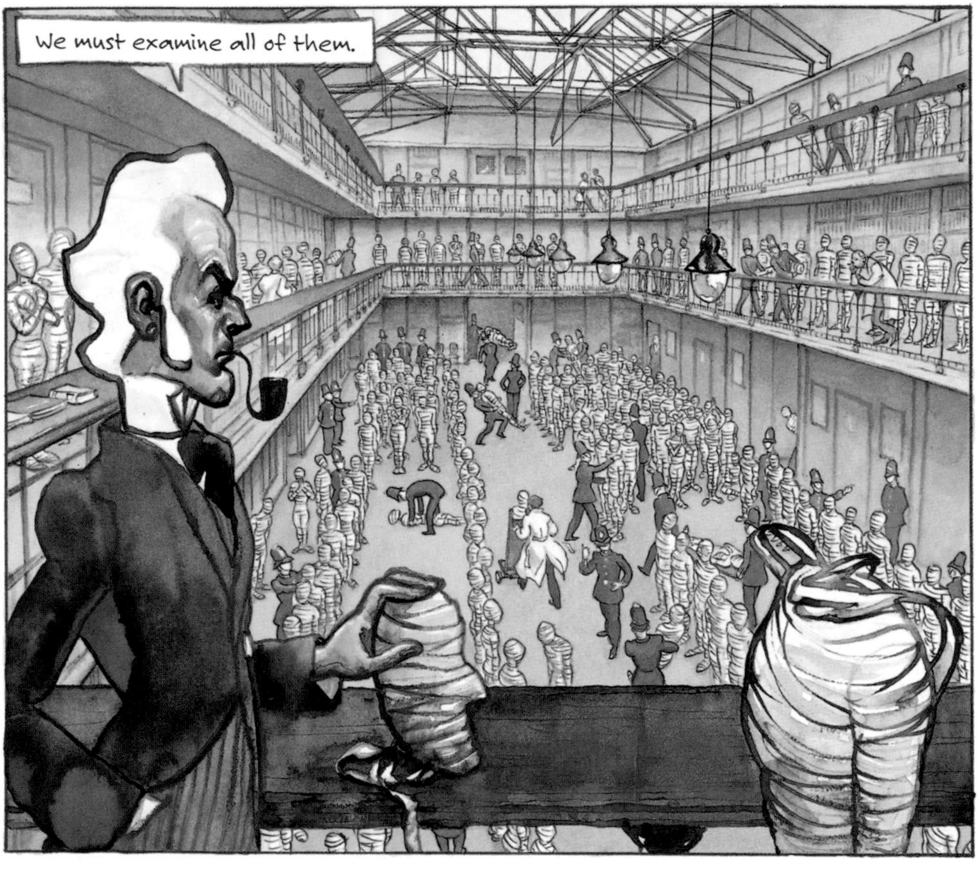
We must examine all of them.

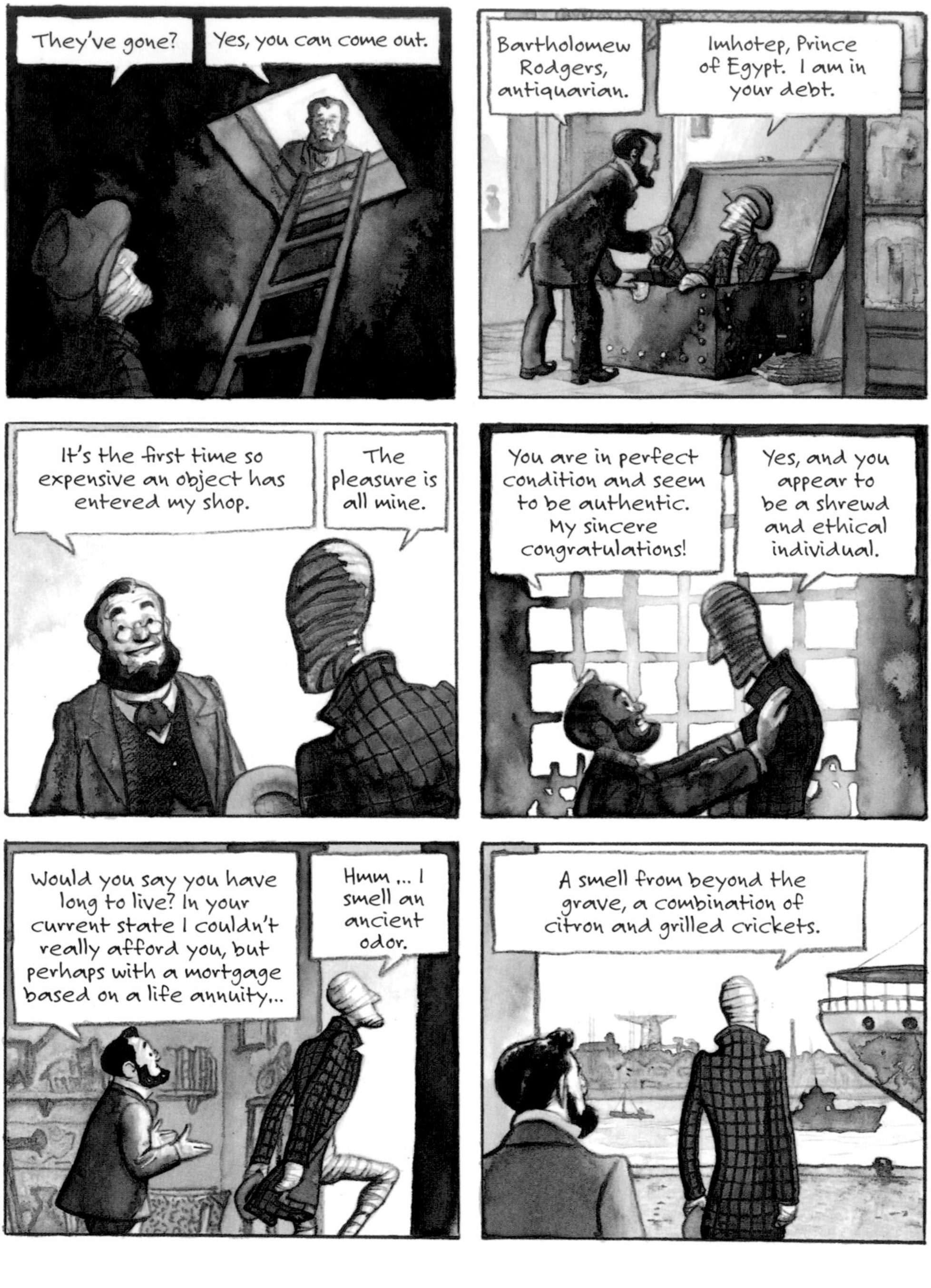
They've gone?
Yes, you can come out.
Bartholomew Rodgers, antiquarian.
Imhotep, Prince of Egypt. I am in your debt.
It's the first time so expensive an object has entered my shop.
The pleasure is all mine.
You are in perfect condition and seem to be authentic. My sincere congratulations!
Yes, and you appear to be a shrewd and ethical individual.
Would you say you have long to live? In your current state I couldn't really afford you, but perhaps with a mortgage based on a life annuity...
Hmm ... I smell an ancient odor.
A smell from beyond the grave, a combination of citron and grilled crickets.

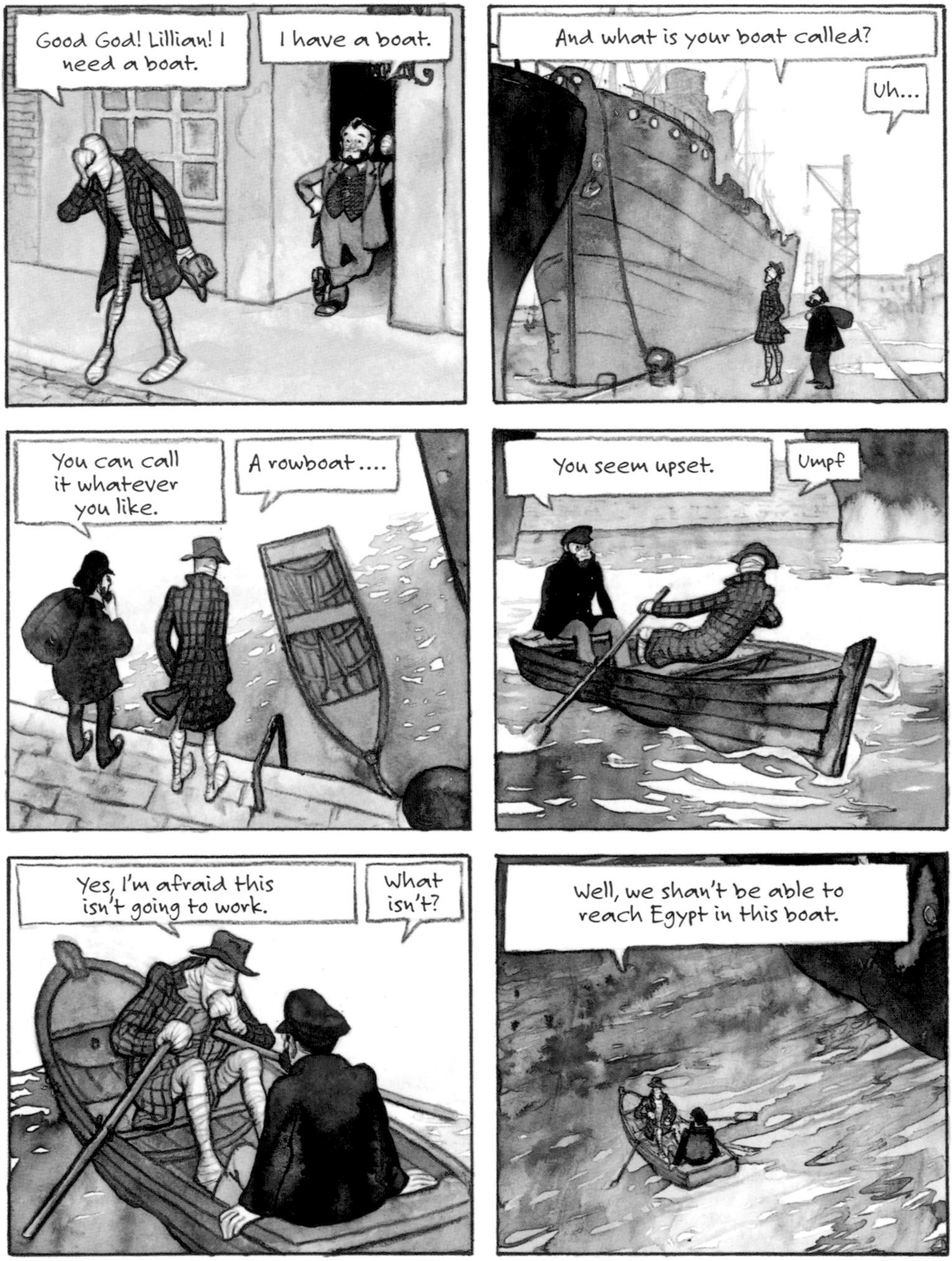
Good God! Lillian! I need a boat.
I have a boat.
And what is your boat called?
Uh...
You can call it whatever you like.
A rowboat....
You seem upset.
Umpf
Yes, I'm afraid this isn't going to work.
What isn't?
Well, we shan't be able to reach Egypt in this boat.

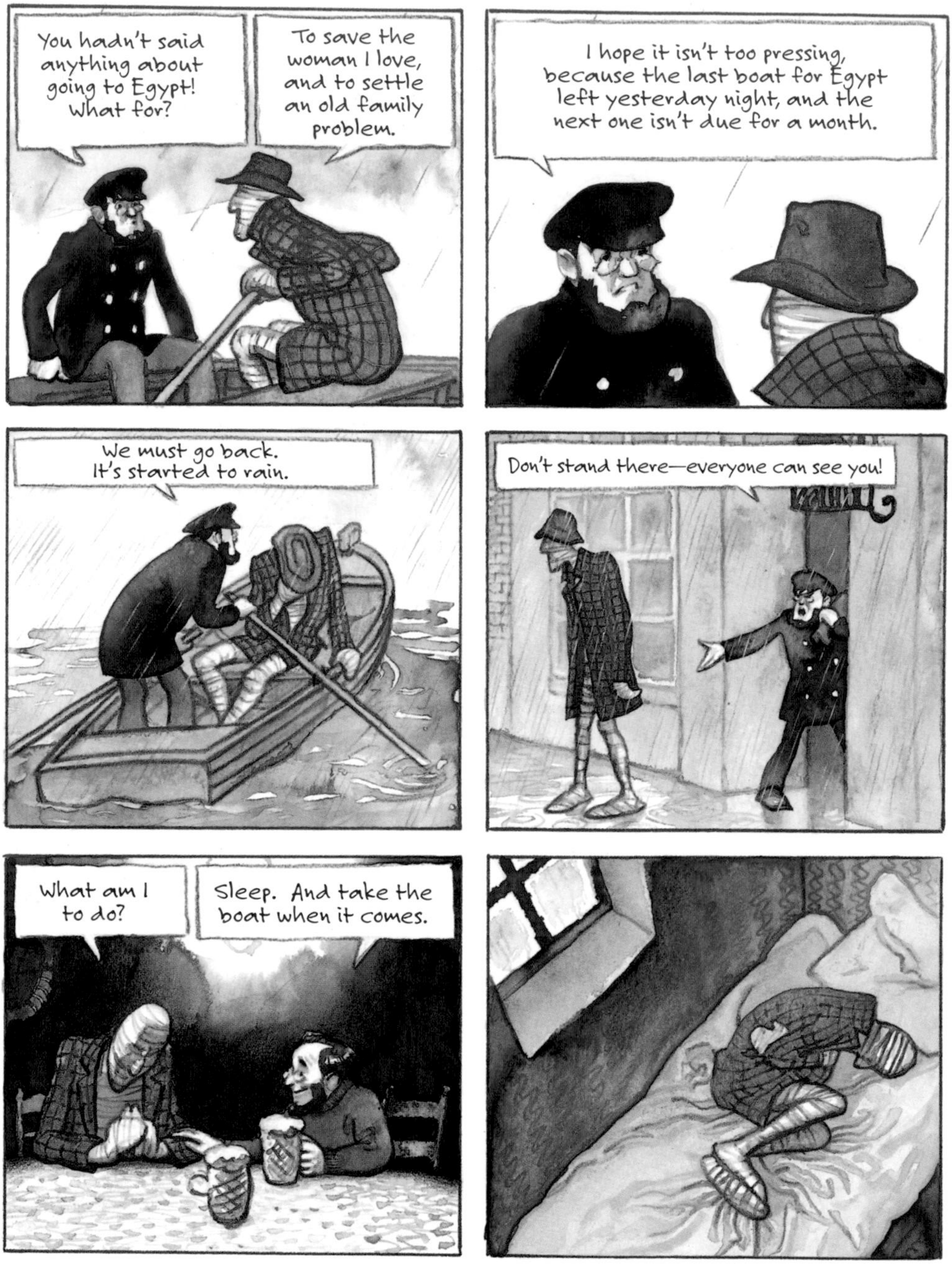
You hadn't said anything about going to Egypt! What for?
To save the woman I love, and to settle an old family problem.
I hope it isn't too pressing, because the last boat for Egypt left yesterday night, and the next one isn't due for a month.
We must go back. It's started to rain.
Don't stand there—everyone can see you!
What am I to do?
Sleep. And take the boat when it comes.

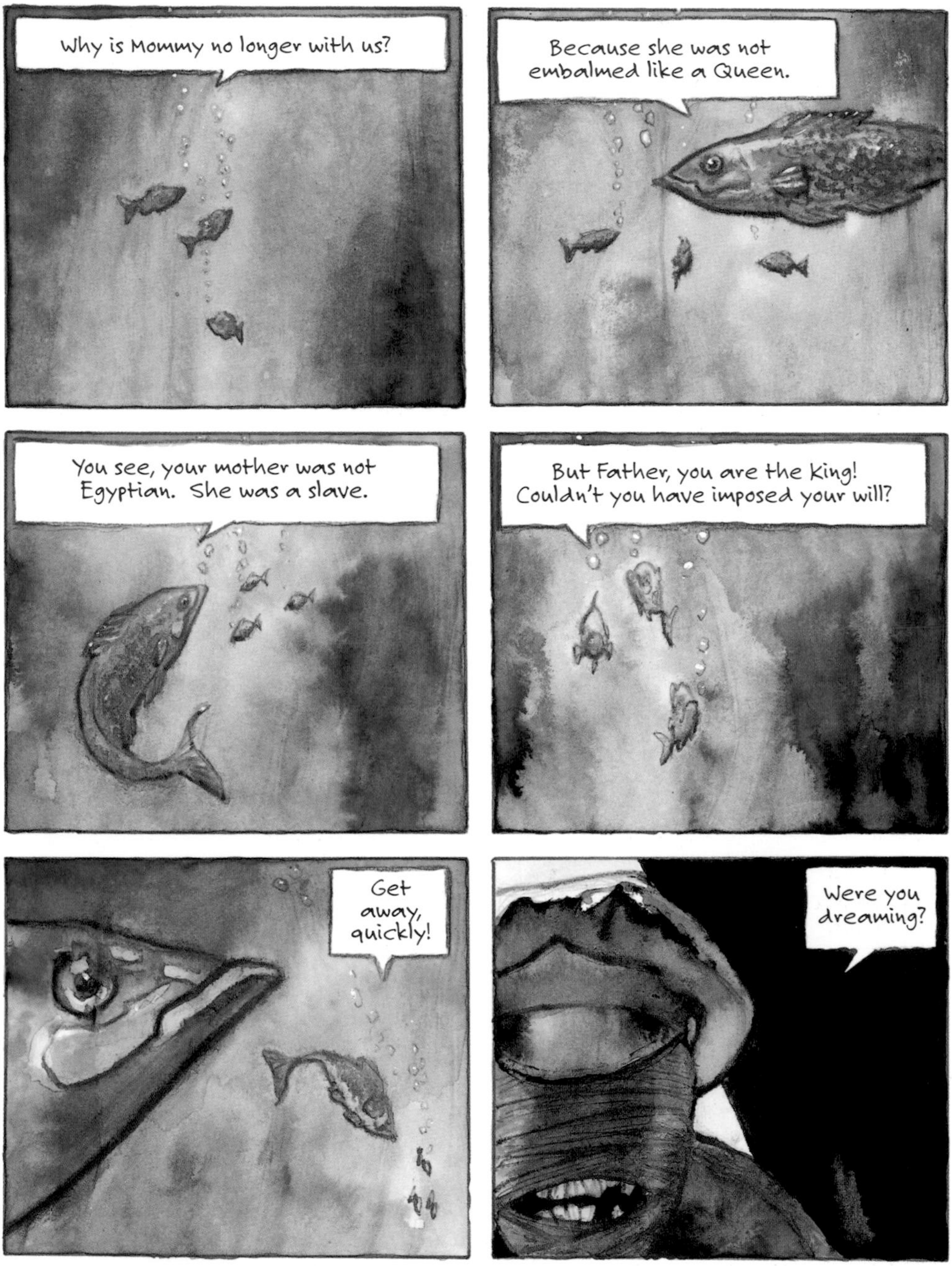
Why is Mommy no longer with us?
Because she was not embalmed like a Queen.
You see, your mother was not Egyptian. She was a slave.
But Father, you are the King! Couldn't you have imposed your will?
Get away, quickly!
Were you dreaming?

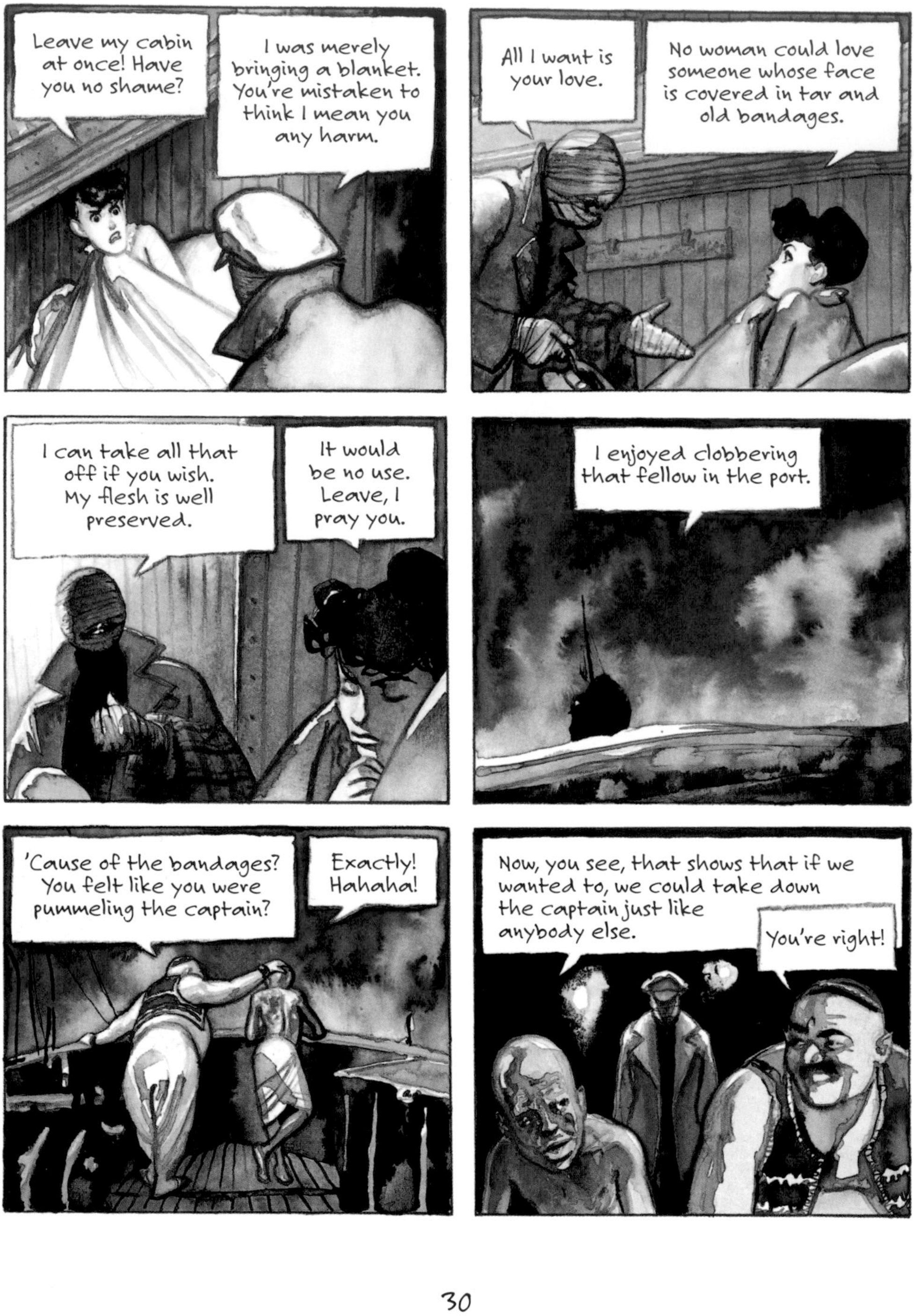
Leave my cabin at once! Have you no shame?
I was merely bringing a blanket. You're mistaken to think I mean you any harm.
All I want is your love.
No woman could love someone whose face is covered in tar and old bandages.
I can take all that off if you wish. My flesh is well preserved.
It would be no use. Leave, I pray you.
I enjoyed clobbering that fellow in the port.
'Cause of the bandages? You felt like you were pummeling the captain?
Exactly! Hahaha!
Now, you see, that shows that if we wanted to, we could take down the captain just like anybody else.
You're right!

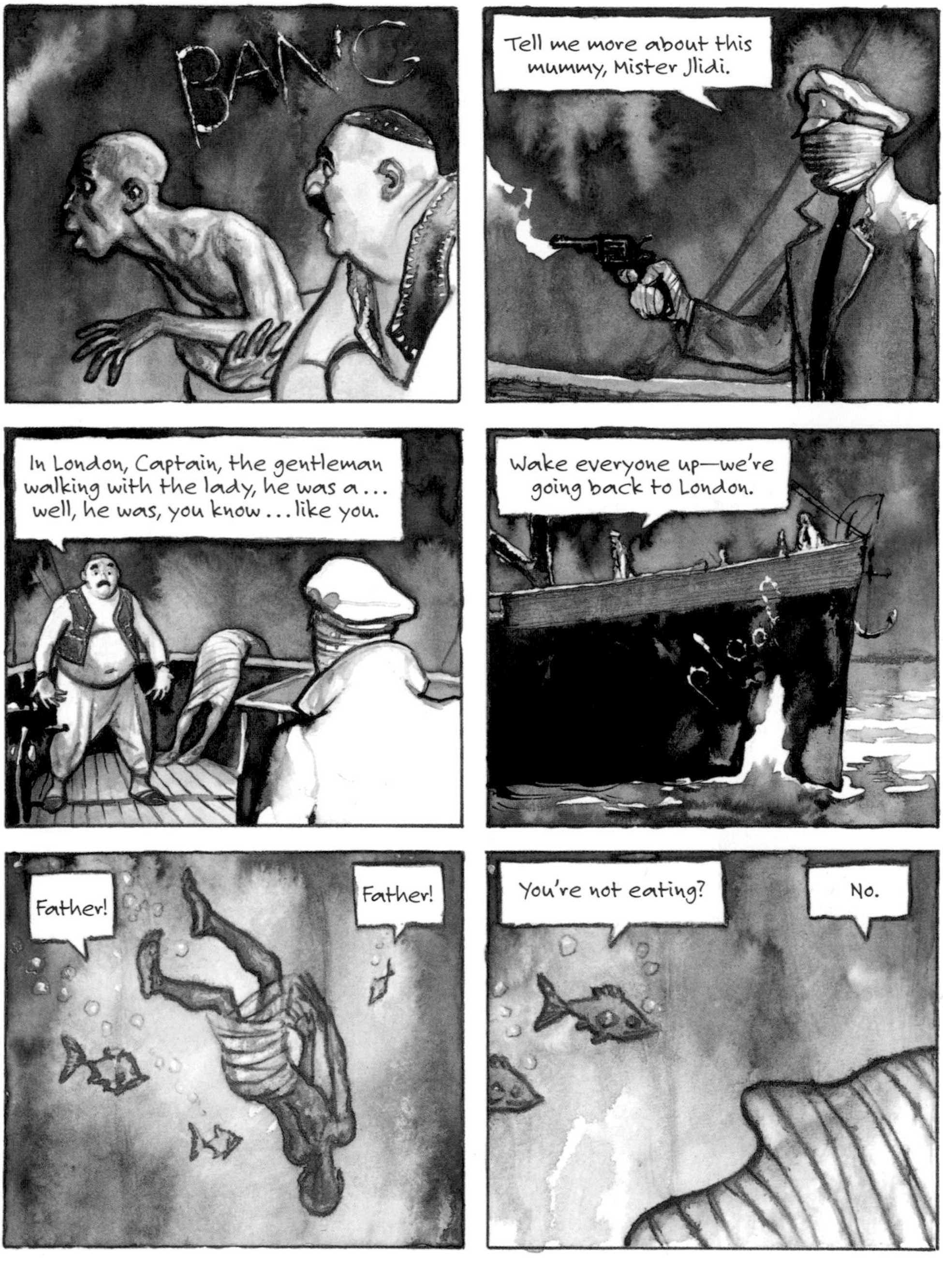
BANG
Tell me more about this mummy, Mister Jlidi.
In London, Captain, the gentleman walking with the lady, he was a . . . well, he was, you know . . . like you.
Wake everyone up—we're going back to London.
Father!
Father!
You're not eating?
No.

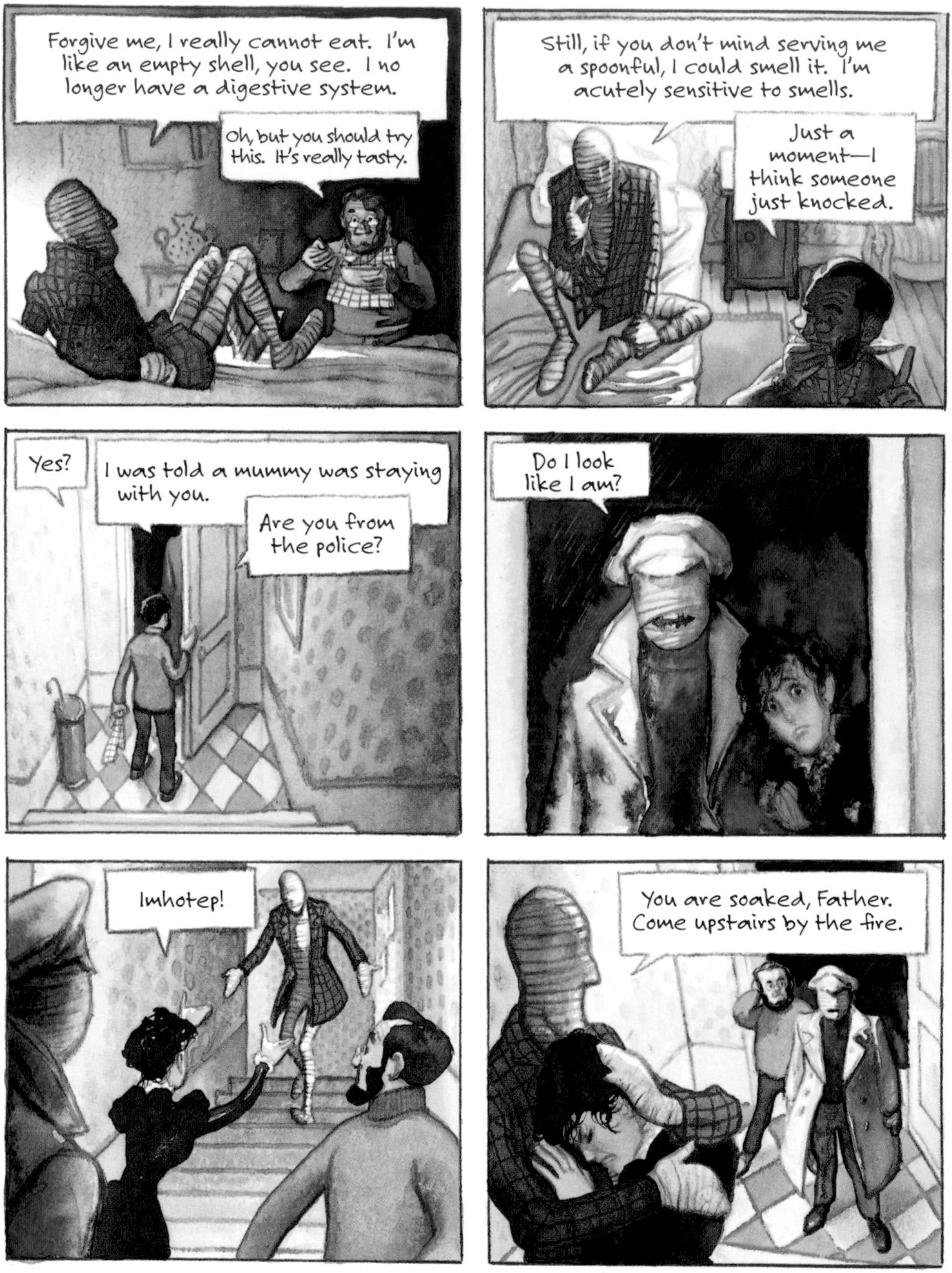
Forgive me, I really cannot eat. I'm like an empty shell, you see. I no longer have a digestive system.
Oh, but you should try this. It's really tasty.
Still, if you don't mind serving me a spoonful, I could smell it. I'm acutely sensitive to smells.
Just a moment—I think someone just knocked.
Yes?
I was told a mummy was staying with you.
Are you from the police?
Do I look like I am?
Imhotep!
You are soaked, Father. Come upstairs by the fire.

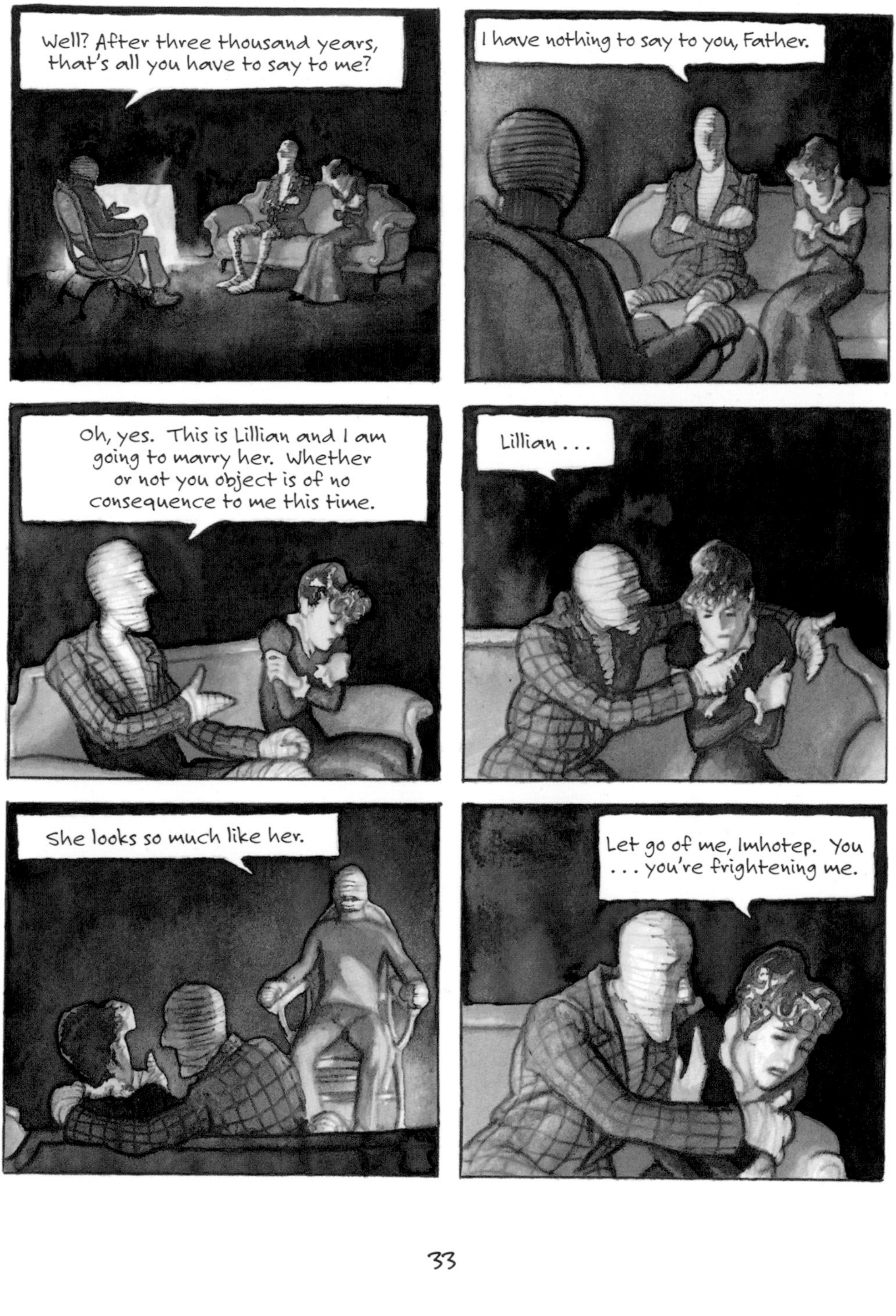
Well? After three thousand years, that's all you have to say to me?
I have nothing to say to you, Father.
Oh, yes. This is Lillian and I am going to marry her. Whether or not you object is of no consequence to me this time.
Lillian . . .
She looks so much like her.
Let go of me, Imhotep. You . . . you're frightening me.

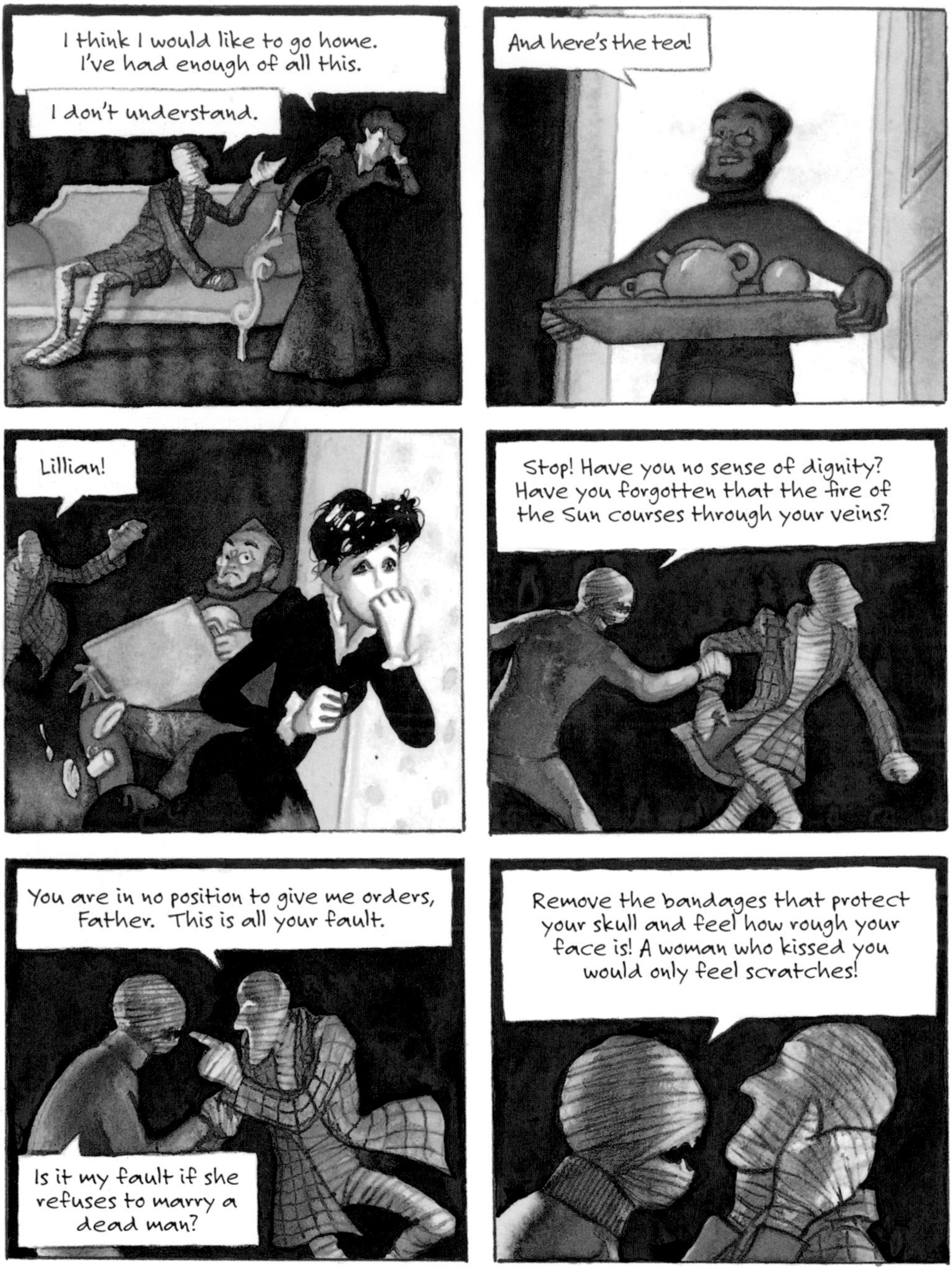
I think I would like to go home. I've had enough of all this.
I don't understand.
And here's the tea!
Lillian!
Stop! Have you no sense of dignity? Have you forgotten that the fire of the Sun courses through your veins?
You are in no position to give me orders, Father. This is all your fault.
Is it my fault if she refuses to marry a dead man?
Remove the bandages that protect your skull and feel how rough your face is! A woman who kissed you would only feel scratches!

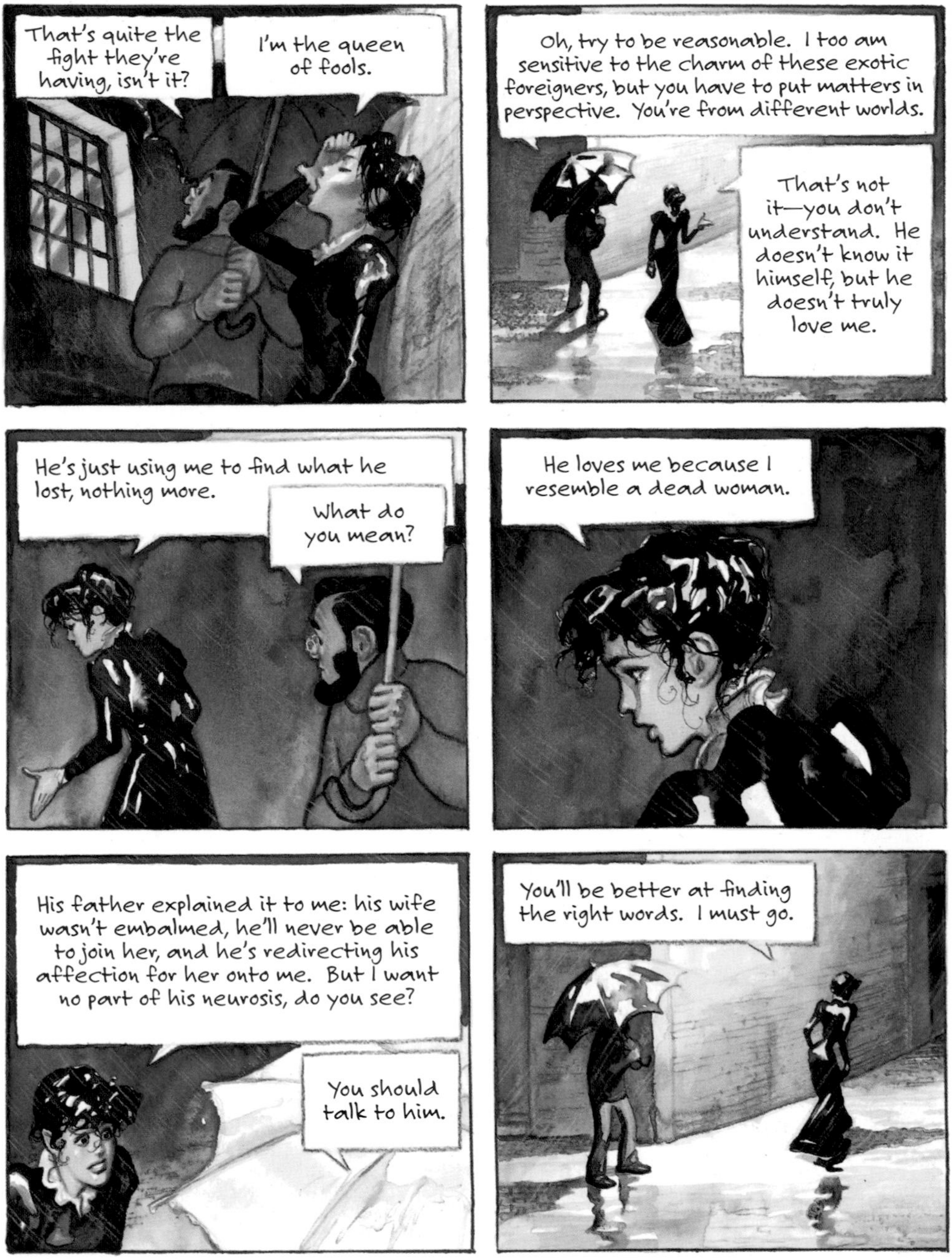
That's quite the fight they're having, isn't it?
I'm the queen of fools.
Oh, try to be reasonable. I too am sensitive to the charm of these exotic foreigners, but you have to put matters in perspective. You're from different worlds.
That's not it—you don't understand. He doesn't know it himself, but he doesn't truly love me.
He's just using me to find what he lost, nothing more.
What do you mean?
He loves me because I resemble a dead woman.
His father explained it to me: his wife wasn't embalmed, he'll never be able to join her, and he's redirecting his affection for her onto me. But I want no part of his neurosis, do you see?
You should talk to him.
You'll be better at finding the right words. I must go.

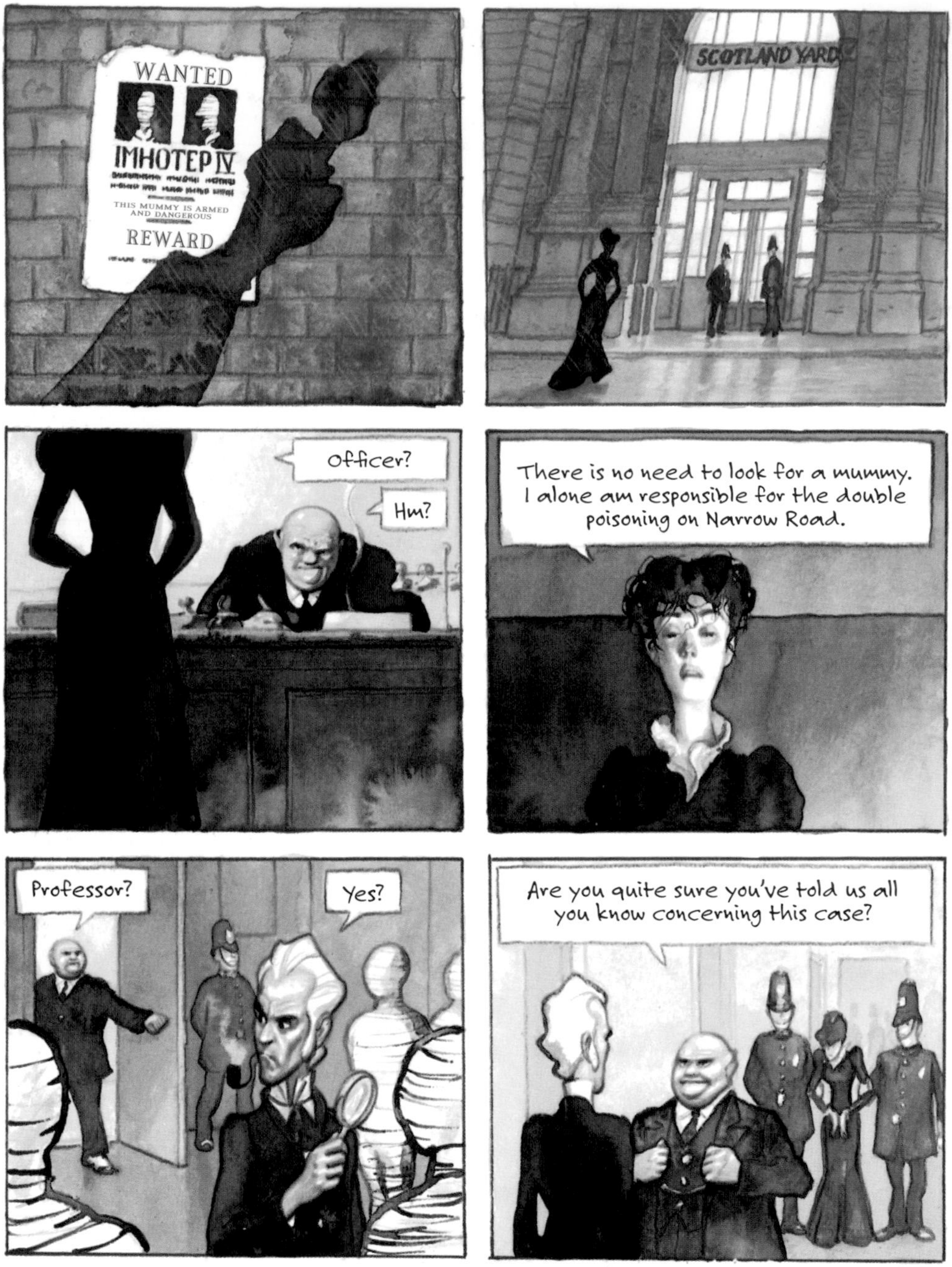

WANTED
IMHOTEP IV
THIS MUMMY IS ARMED AND DANGEROUS
REWARD
SCOTLAND YARD
Officer?
Hm?
There is no need to look for a mummy. I alone am responsible for the double poisoning on Narrow Road.
Professor?
Yes?
Are you quite sure you've told us all you know concerning this case?

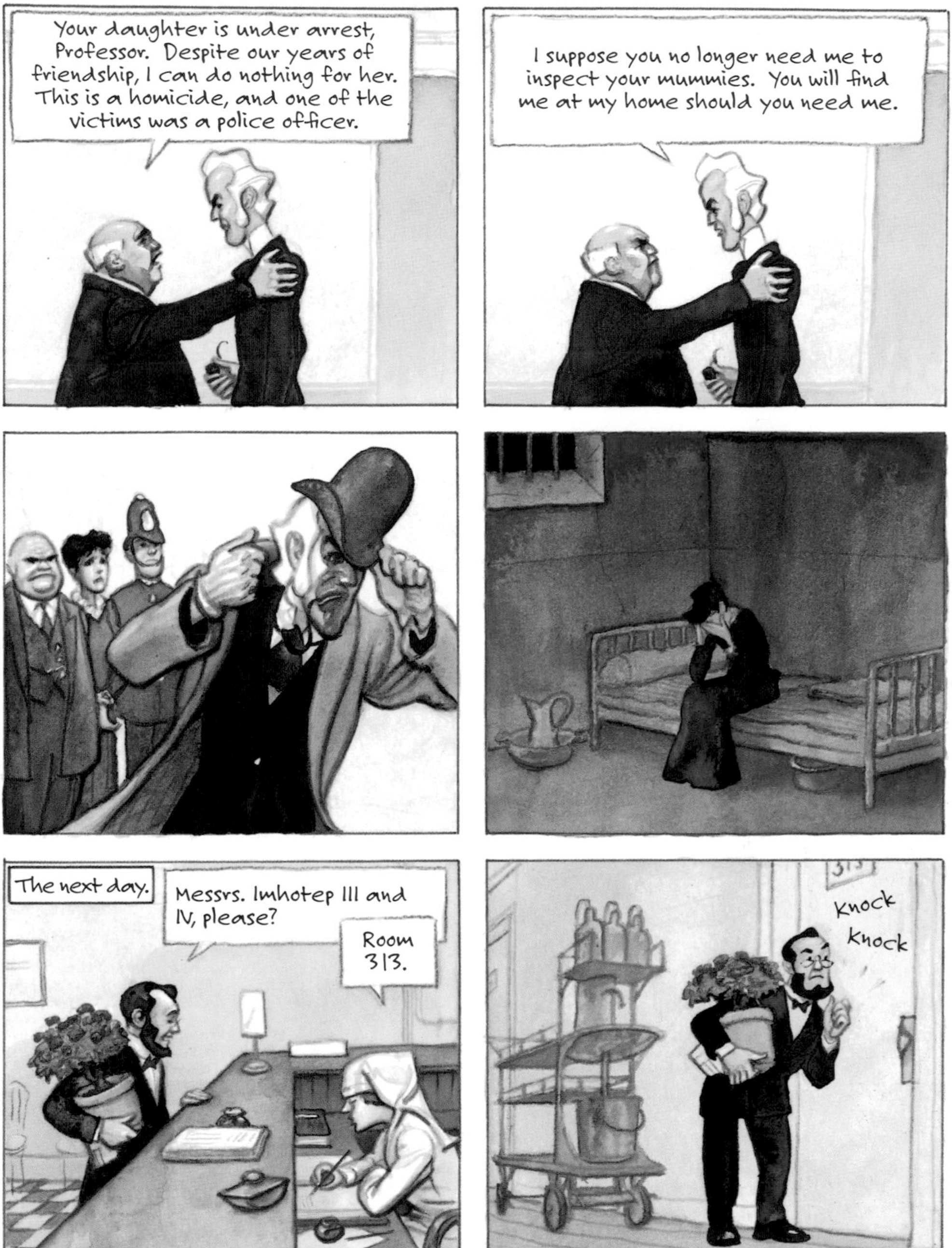
Your daughter is under arrest, Professor. Despite our years of friendship, I can do nothing for her. This is a homicide, and one of the victims was a police officer.
I suppose you no longer need me to inspect your mummies. You will find me at my home should you need me.
The next day.
Messrs. Imhotep III and IV, please?
Room 313.
Knock
Knock

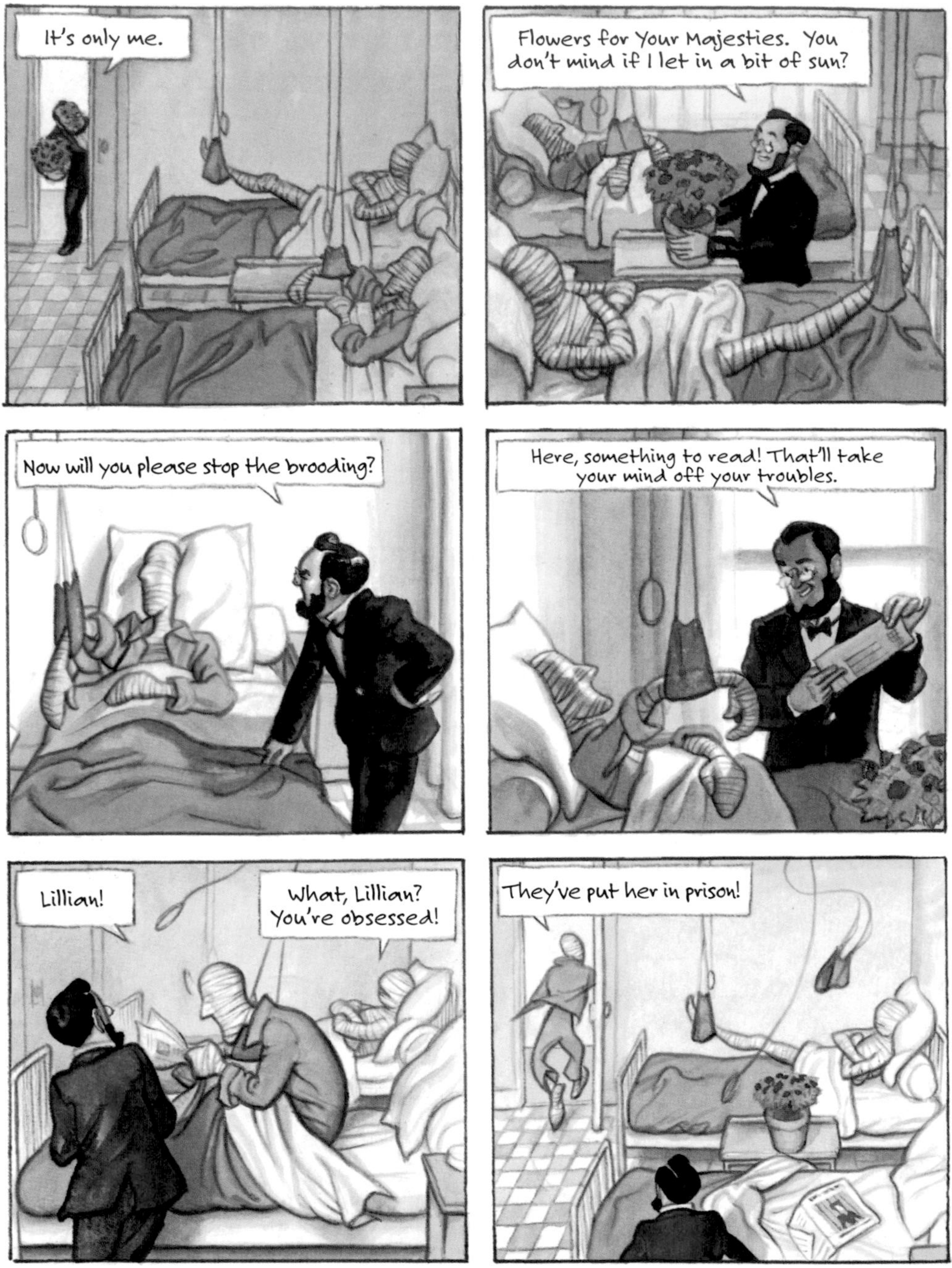
It's only me.
Flowers for Your Majesties. You don't mind if I let in a bit of sun?
Now will you please stop the brooding?
Here, something to read! That'll take your mind off your troubles.
Lillian!
What, Lillian? You're obsessed!
They've put her in prison!

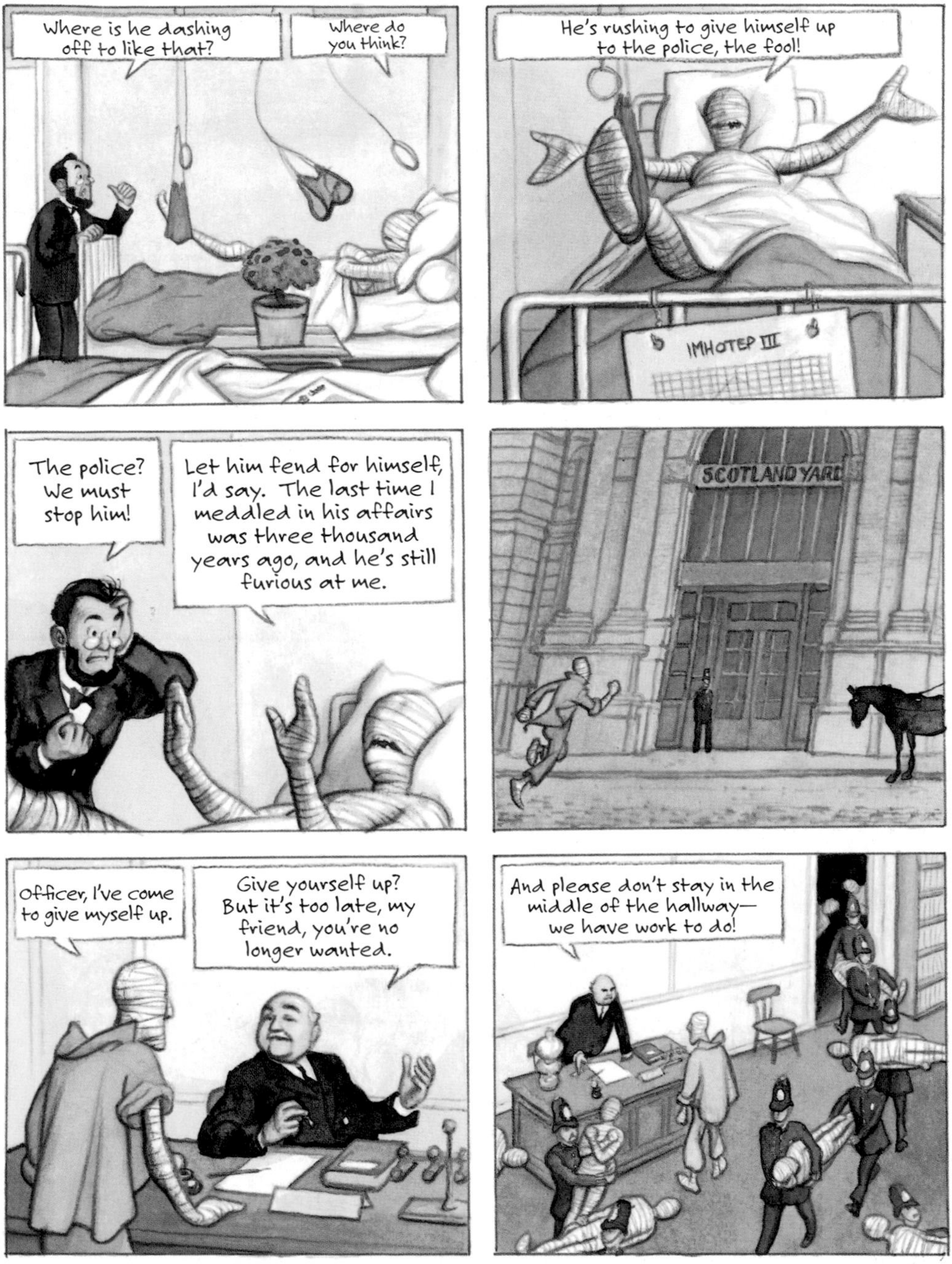
Where is he dashing off to like that?
Where do you think?
He's rushing to give himself up to the police, the fool!
IMHOTEP III
The police? We must stop him!
Let him fend for himself, I'd say. The last time I meddled in his affairs was three thousand years ago, and he's still furious at me.
SCOTLAND YARD
Officer, I've come to give myself up.
Give yourself up? But it's too late, my friend, you're no longer wanted.
And please don't stay in the middle of the hallway— we have work to do!

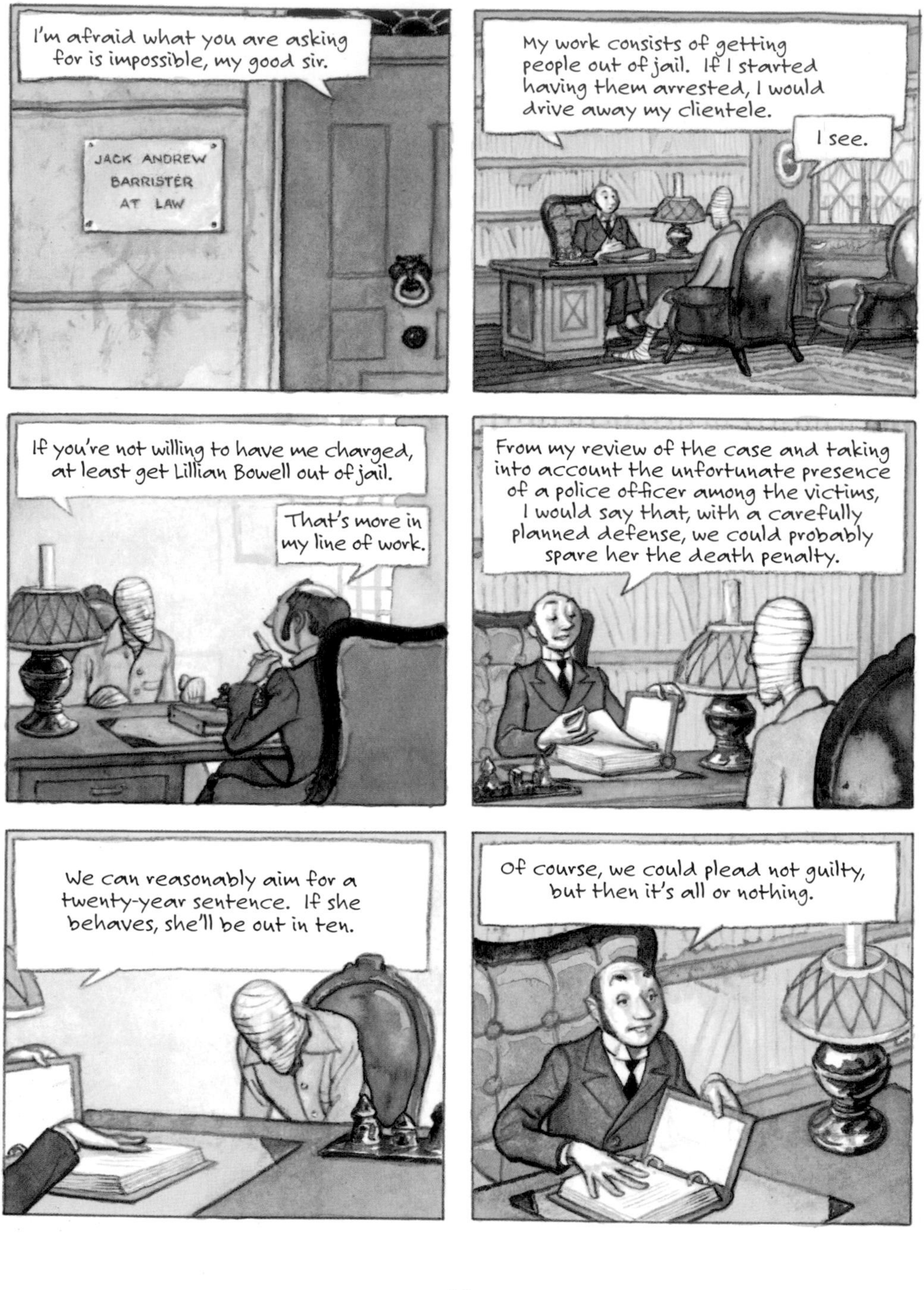
I'm afraid what you are asking for is impossible, my good sir.
JACK ANDREW BARRISTER AT LAW
My work consists of getting people out of jail. If I started having them arrested, I would drive away my clientele.
I see.
If you're not willing to have me charged, at least get Lillian Bowell out of jail.
That's more in my line of work.
From my review of the case and taking into account the unfortunate presence of a police officer among the victims, I would say that, with a carefully planned defense, we could probably spare her the death penalty.
We can reasonably aim for a twenty-year sentence. If she behaves, she'll be out in ten.
Of course, we could plead not guilty, but then it's all or nothing.

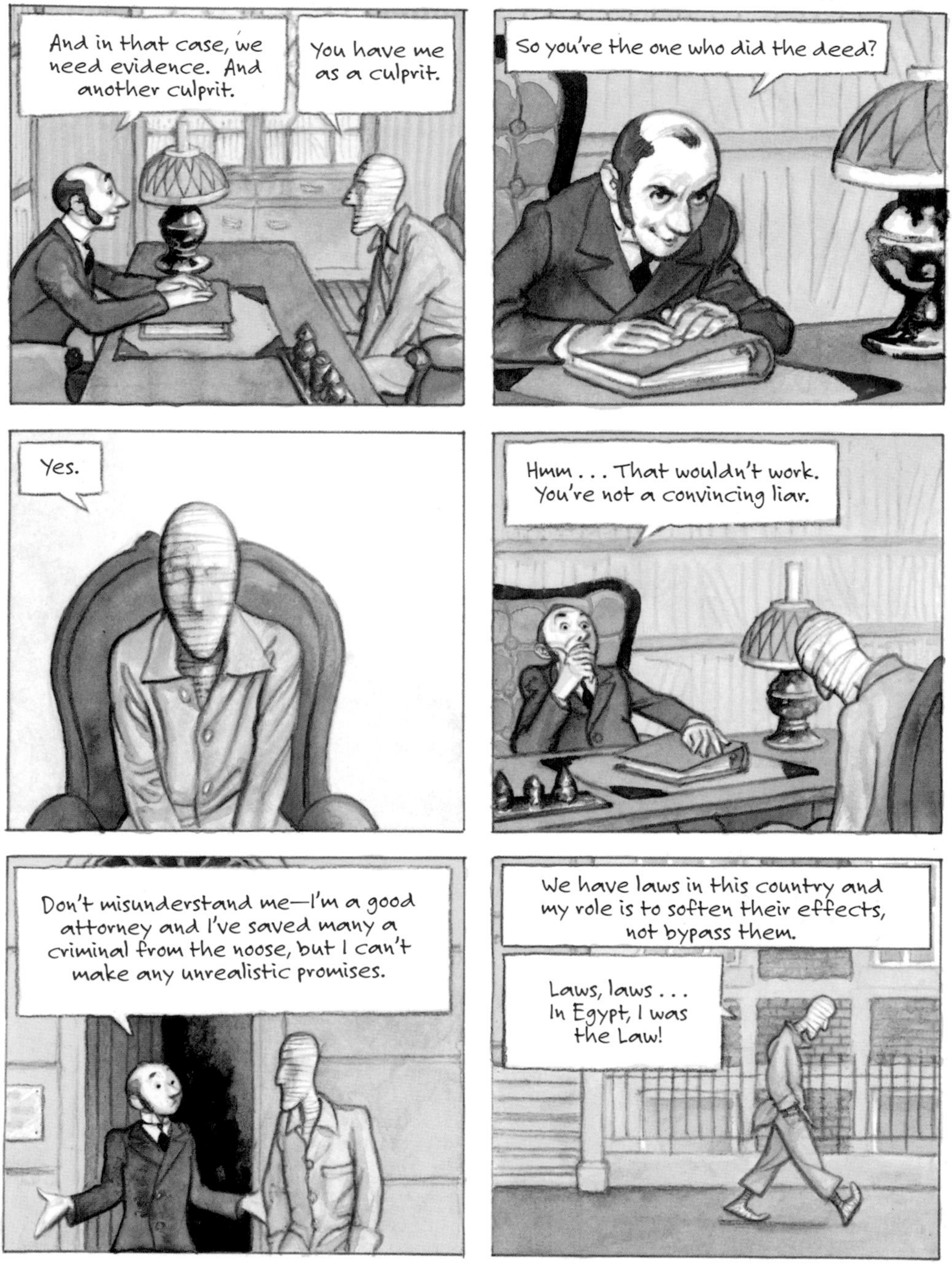
And in that case, we need evidence. And another culprit.
You have me as a culprit.
So you're the one who did the deed?
Yes.
Hmm . . . That wouldn't work. You're not a convincing liar.
Don't misunderstand me—I'm a good attorney and I've saved many a criminal from the noose, but I can't make any unrealistic promises.
We have laws in this country and my role is to soften their effects, not bypass them.
Laws, laws . . . In Egypt, I was the Law!

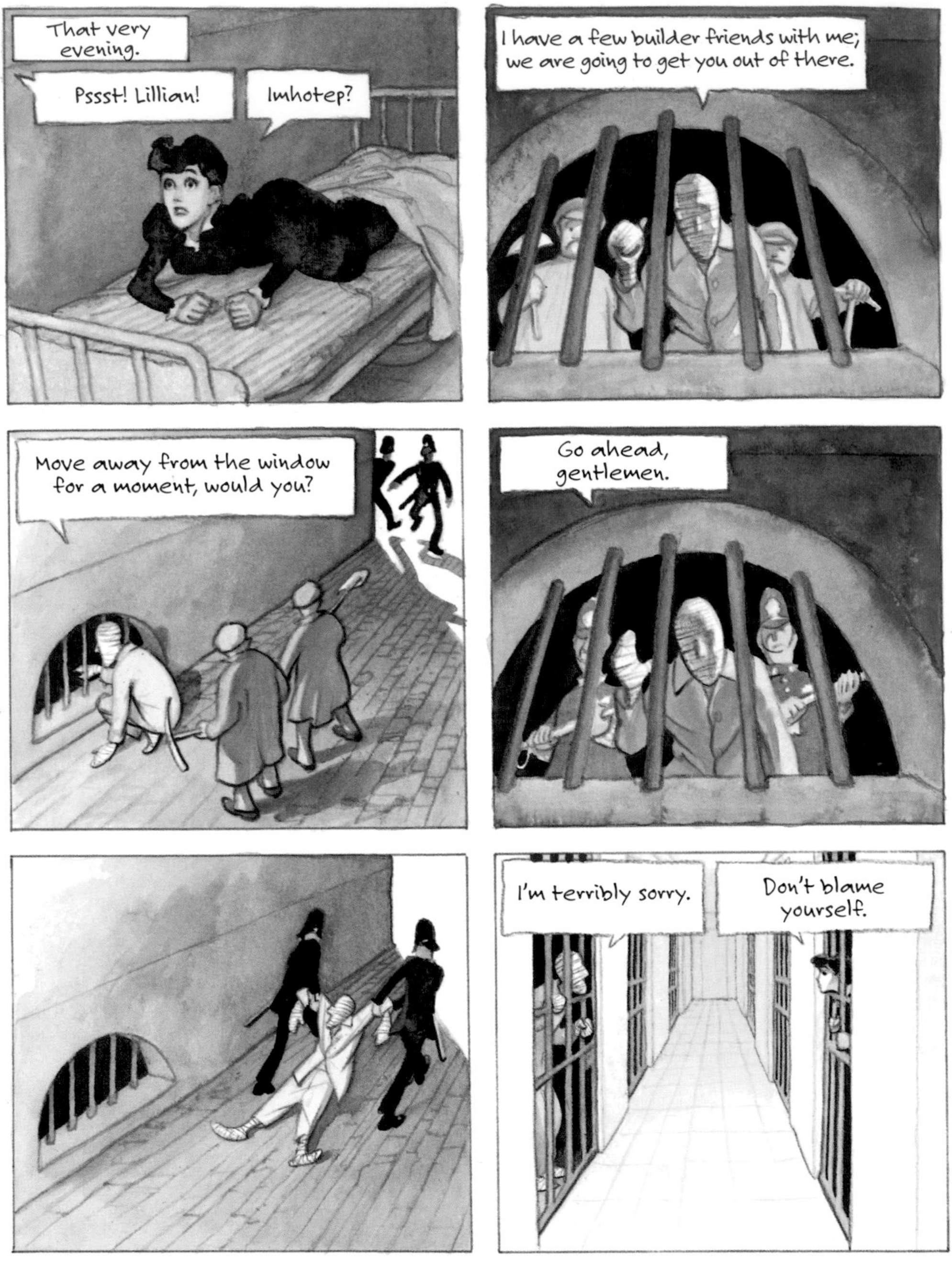
That very evening.
Pssst! Lillian!
Imhotep?
I have a few builder friends with me; we are going to get you out of there.
Move away from the window for a moment, would you?
Go ahead, gentlemen.
I'm terribly sorry.
Don't blame yourself.

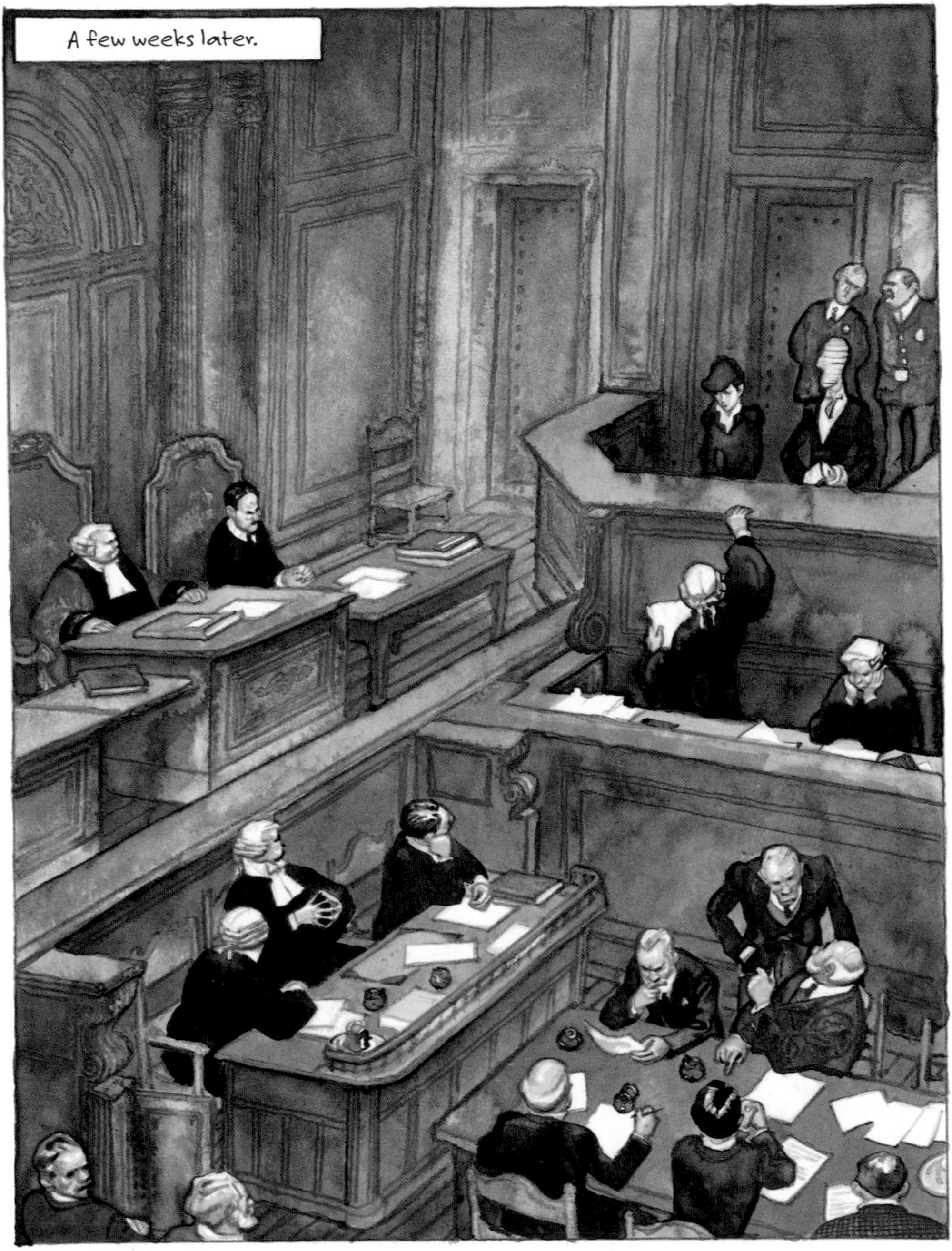

A few weeks later.

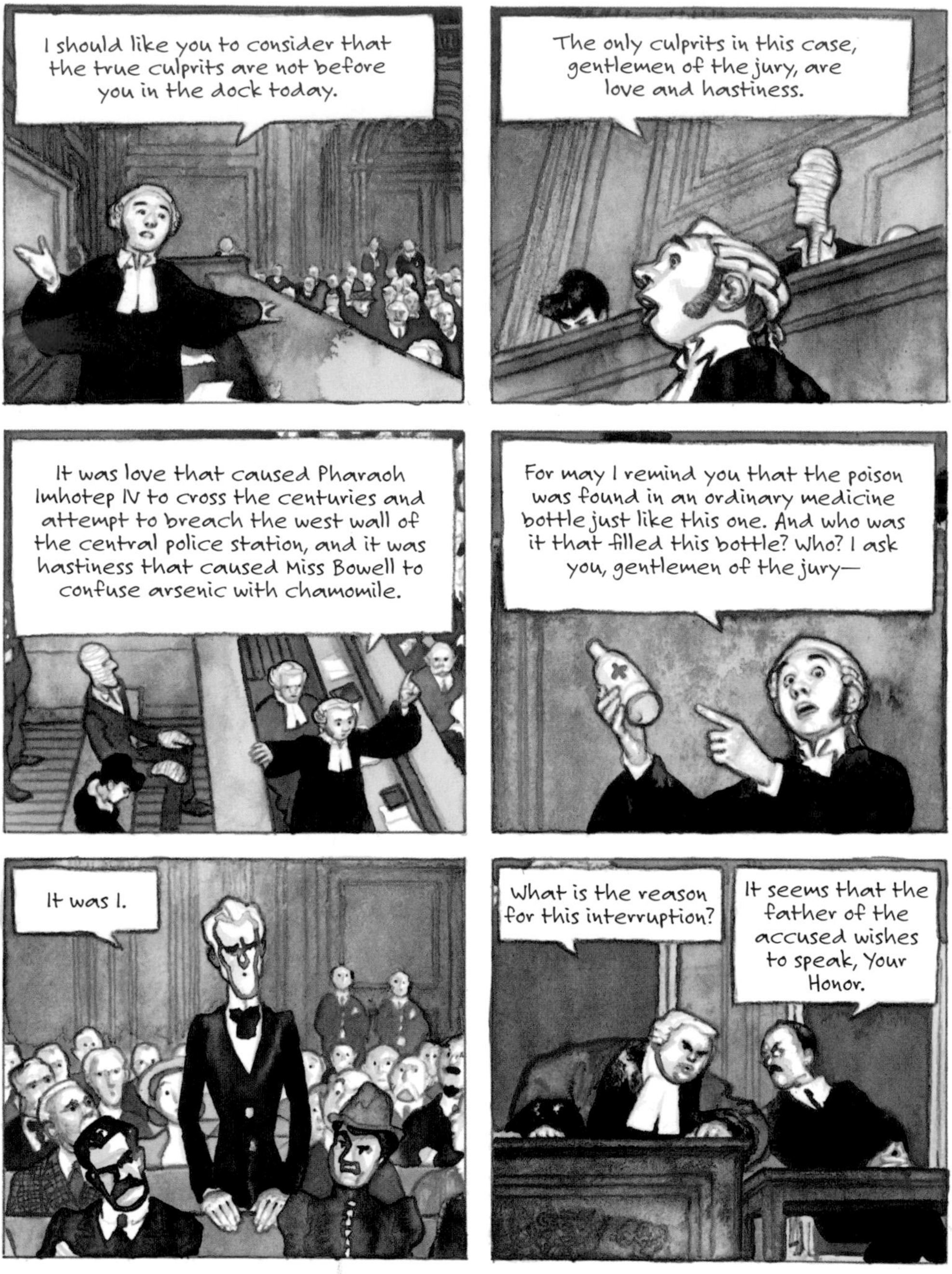
I should like you to consider that the true culprits are not before you in the dock today.
The only culprits in this case, gentlemen of the jury, are love and hastiness.
It was love that caused Pharaoh Imhotep IV to cross the centuries and attempt to breach the west wall of the central police station, and it was hastiness that caused Miss Bowell to confuse arsenic with chamomile.
For may I remind you that the poison was found in an ordinary medicine bottle just like this one. And who was it that filled this bottle? Who? I ask you, gentlemen of the jury—
It was I.
What is the reason for this interruption?
It seems that the father of the accused wishes to speak, Your Honor.

I am currently writing a treatise on poisons and my samples were lying about. My daughter was unaware of this.

Objection, Your Honor!

The Prosecution has the floor.

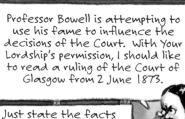

Professor Bowell is attempting to use his fame to influence the decisions of the Court. With Your Lordship's permission, I should like to read a ruling of the Court of Glasgow from 2 June 1873.

Just state the facts of the case.

The facts are simple. A housemaid had served adulterated milk to her masters, causing them to die. It was proved that the accused was unaware that the product was harmful. Nevertheless, she was convicted and hanged.

I do not want the courts of the realm to condemn the poor and acquit the wealthy, Your Honor. If this trial is to set an example, it should be one of firmness, not of indulgence for the upper classes.

That is why, irrespective of Professor Bowell's tearful intervention, my findings stand. I call for the noose for Miss Bowell and the museum display case for her associate.

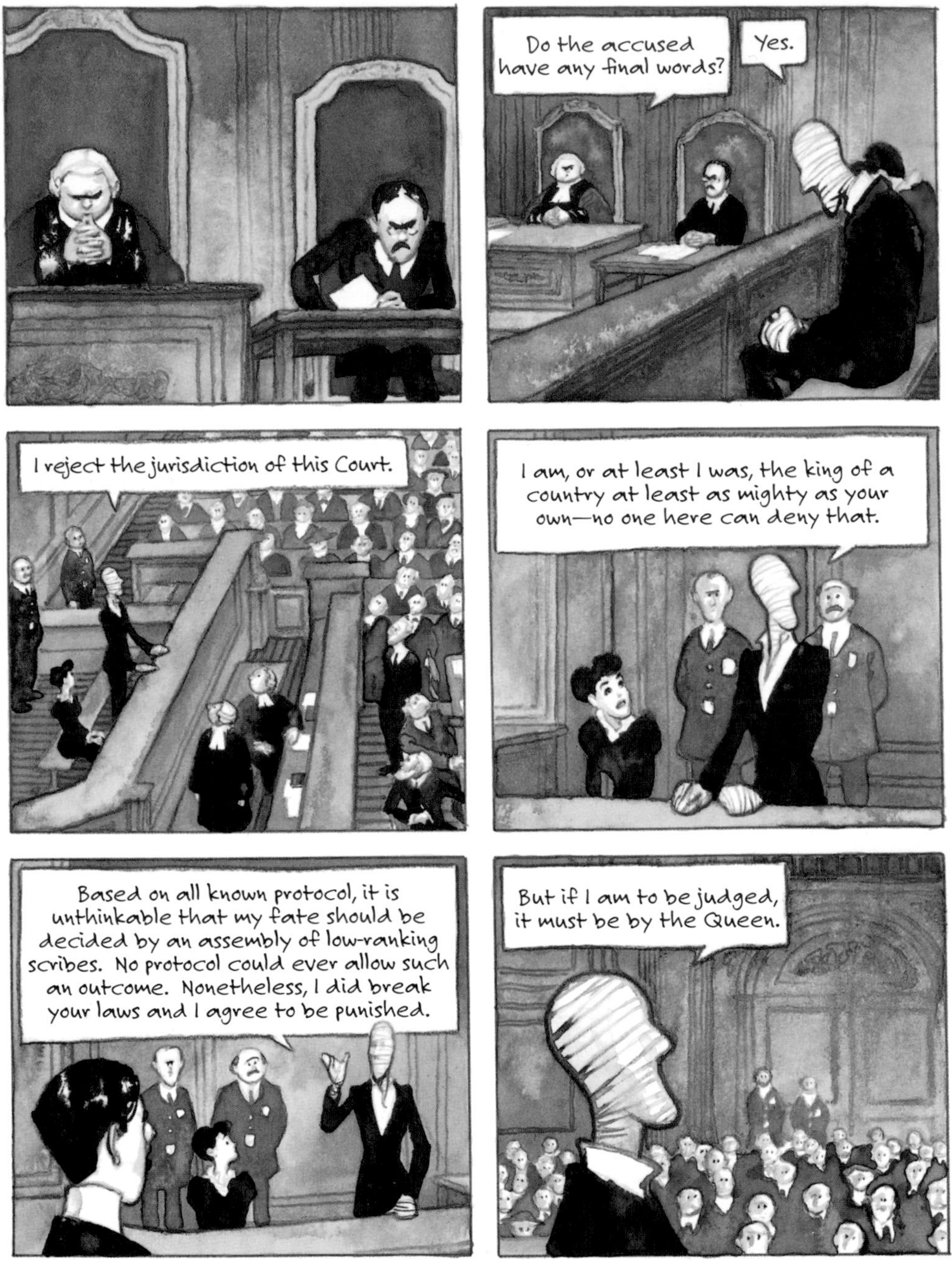
Do the accused have any final words?
Yes.
I reject the jurisdiction of this Court.
I am, or at least I was, the king of a country at least as mighty as your own—no one here can deny that.
Based on all known protocol, it is unthinkable that my fate should be decided by an assembly of low-ranking scribes. No protocol could ever allow such an outcome. Nonetheless, I did break your laws and I agree to be punished.
But if I am to be judged, it must be by the Queen.

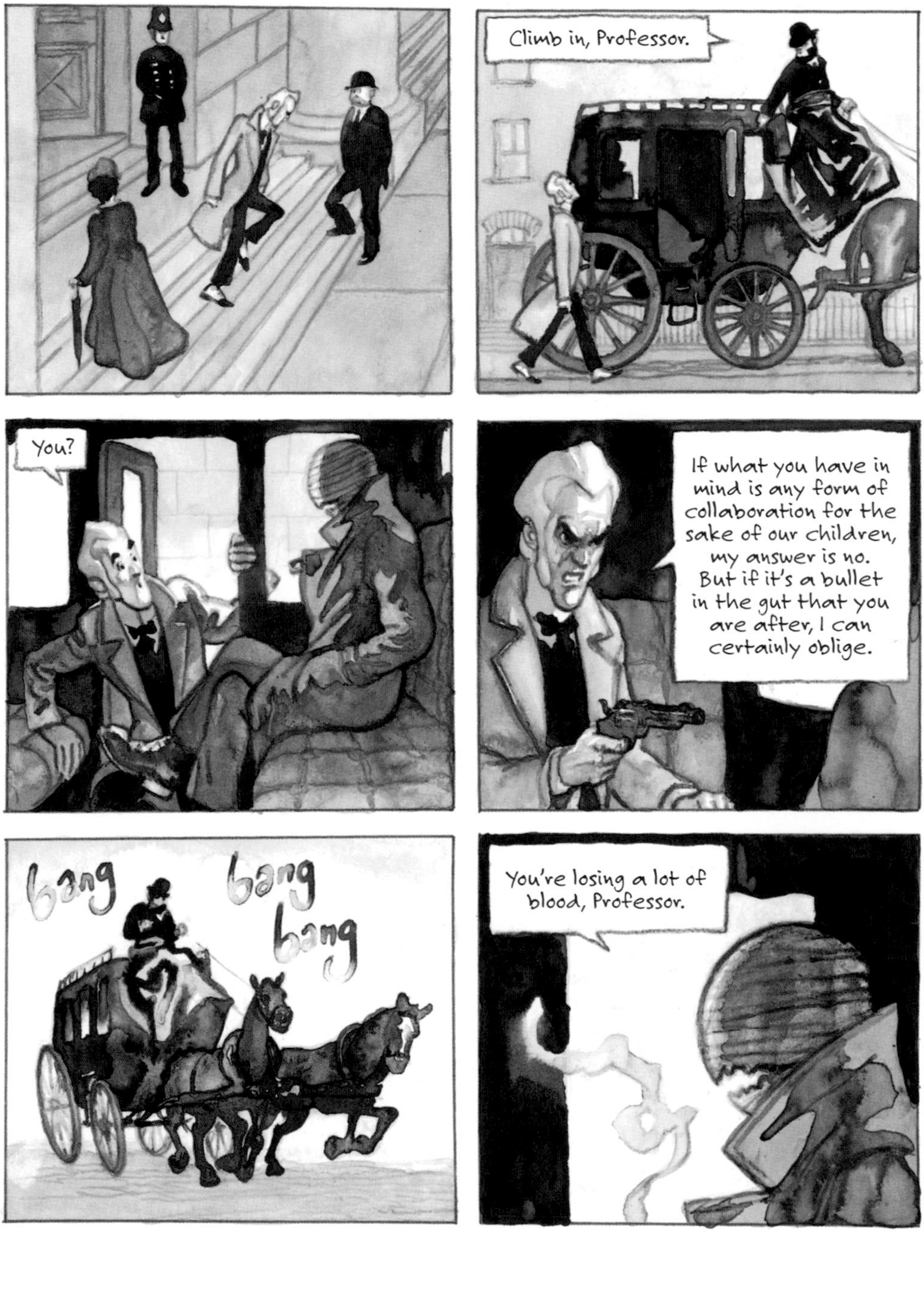
Climb in, Professor.
You?
If what you have in mind is any form of collaboration for the sake of our children, my answer is no. But if it's a bullet in the gut that you are after, I can certainly oblige.
bang bang bang
You're losing a lot of blood, Professor.

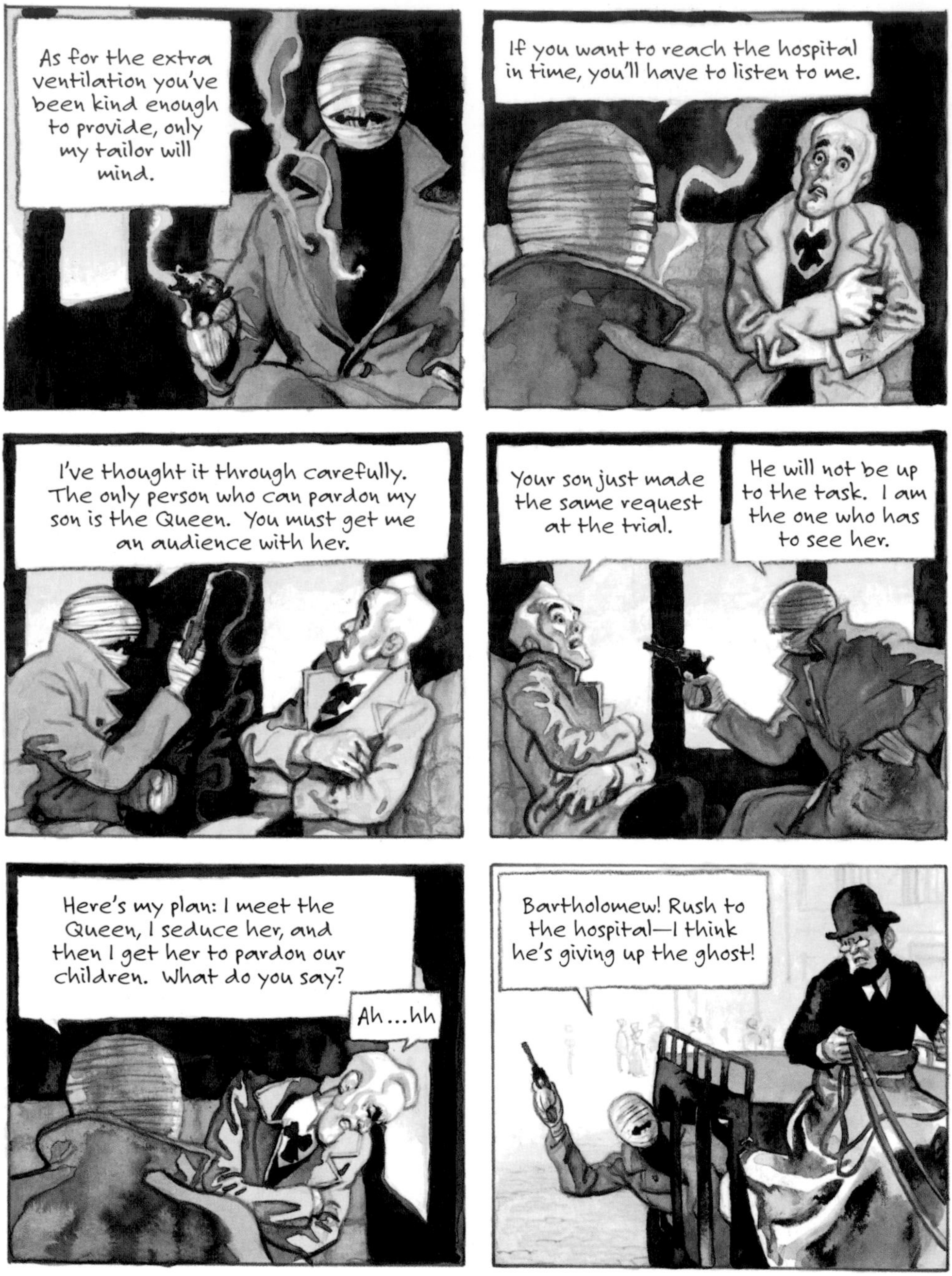
As for the extra ventilation you've been kind enough to provide, only my tailor will mind.
If you want to reach the hospital in time, you'll have to listen to me.
I've thought it through carefully. The only person who can pardon my son is the Queen. You must get me an audience with her.
Your son just made the same request at the trial.
He will not be up to the task. I am the one who has to see her.
Here's my plan: I meet the Queen, I seduce her, and then I get her to pardon our children. What do you say?
Ah...hh
Bartholomew! Rush to the hospital—I think he's giving up the ghost!

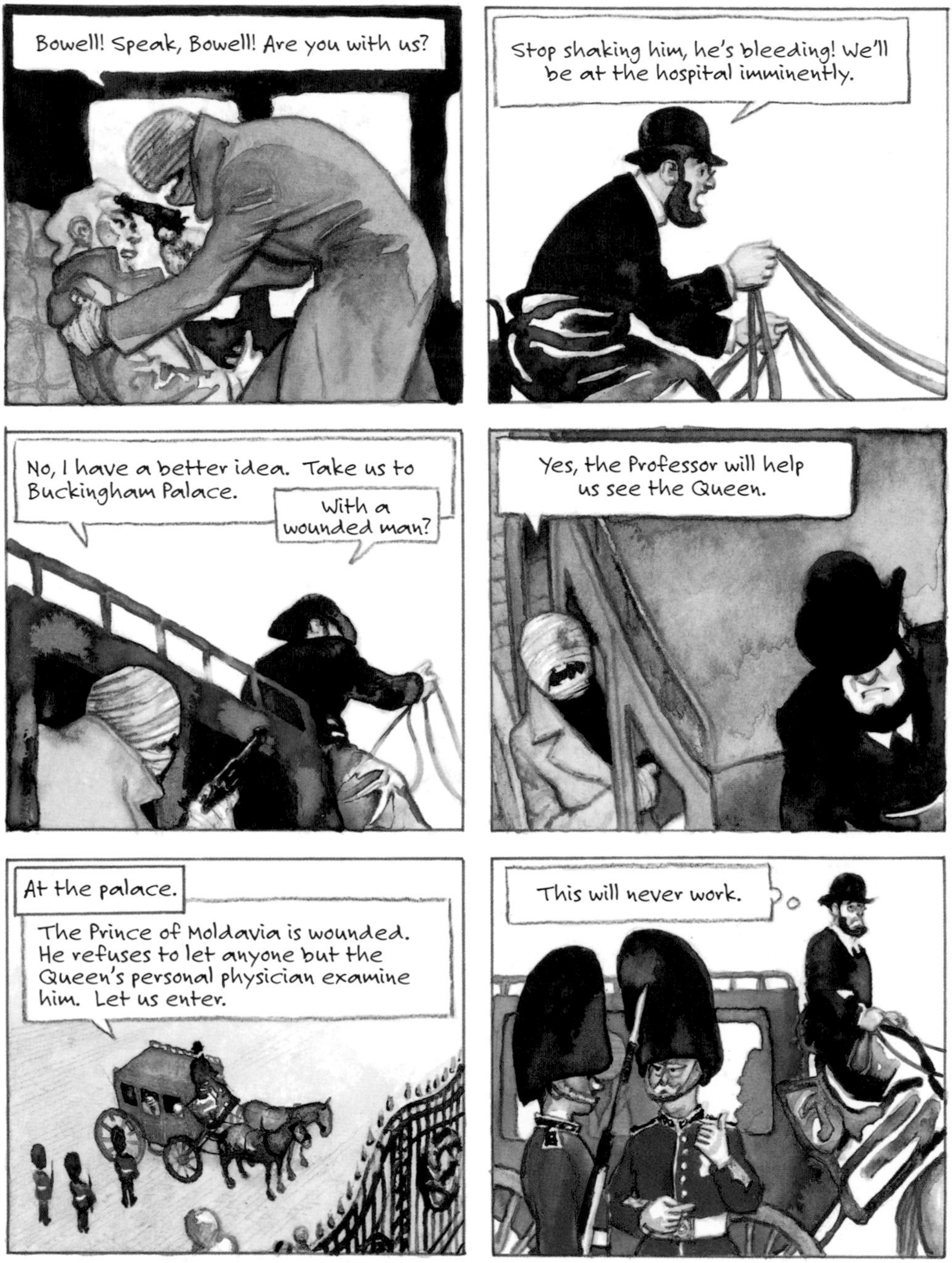
Bowell! Speak, Bowell! Are you with us?
Stop shaking him, he's bleeding! We'll be at the hospital imminently.
No, I have a better idea. Take us to Buckingham Palace.
With a wounded man?
Yes, the Professor will help us see the Queen.
At the palace.
The Prince of Moldavia is wounded. He refuses to let anyone but the Queen's personal physician examine him. Let us enter.
This will never work.

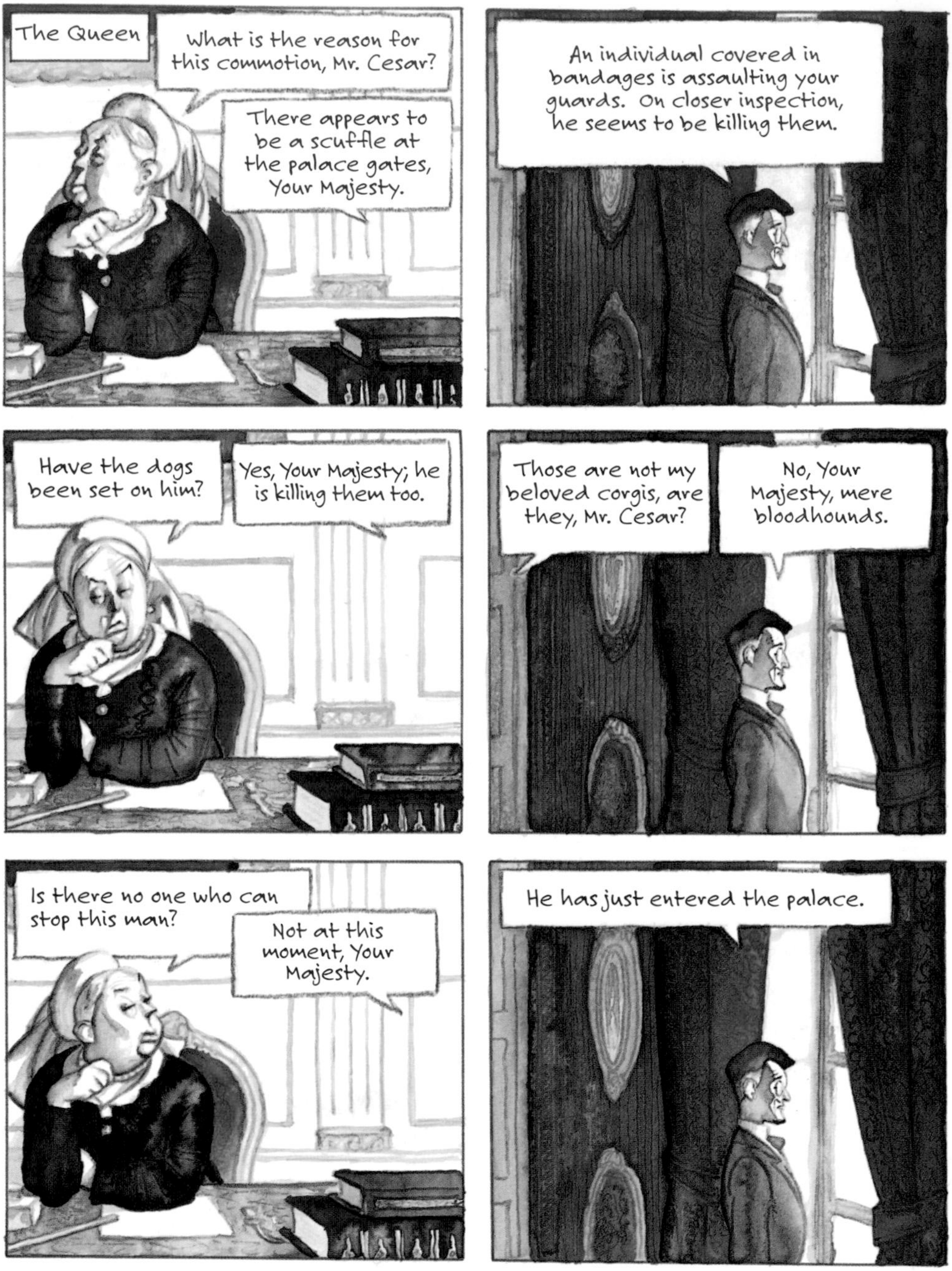
The Queen
What is the reason for this commotion, Mr. Cesar?
There appears to be a scuffle at the palace gates, Your Majesty.
An individual covered in bandages is assaulting your guards. On closer inspection, he seems to be killing them.
Have the dogs been set on him?
Yes, Your Majesty; he is killing them too.
Those are not my beloved corgis, are they, Mr. Cesar?
No, Your Majesty, mere bloodhounds.
Is there no one who can stop this man?
Not at this moment, Your Majesty.
He has just entered the palace.

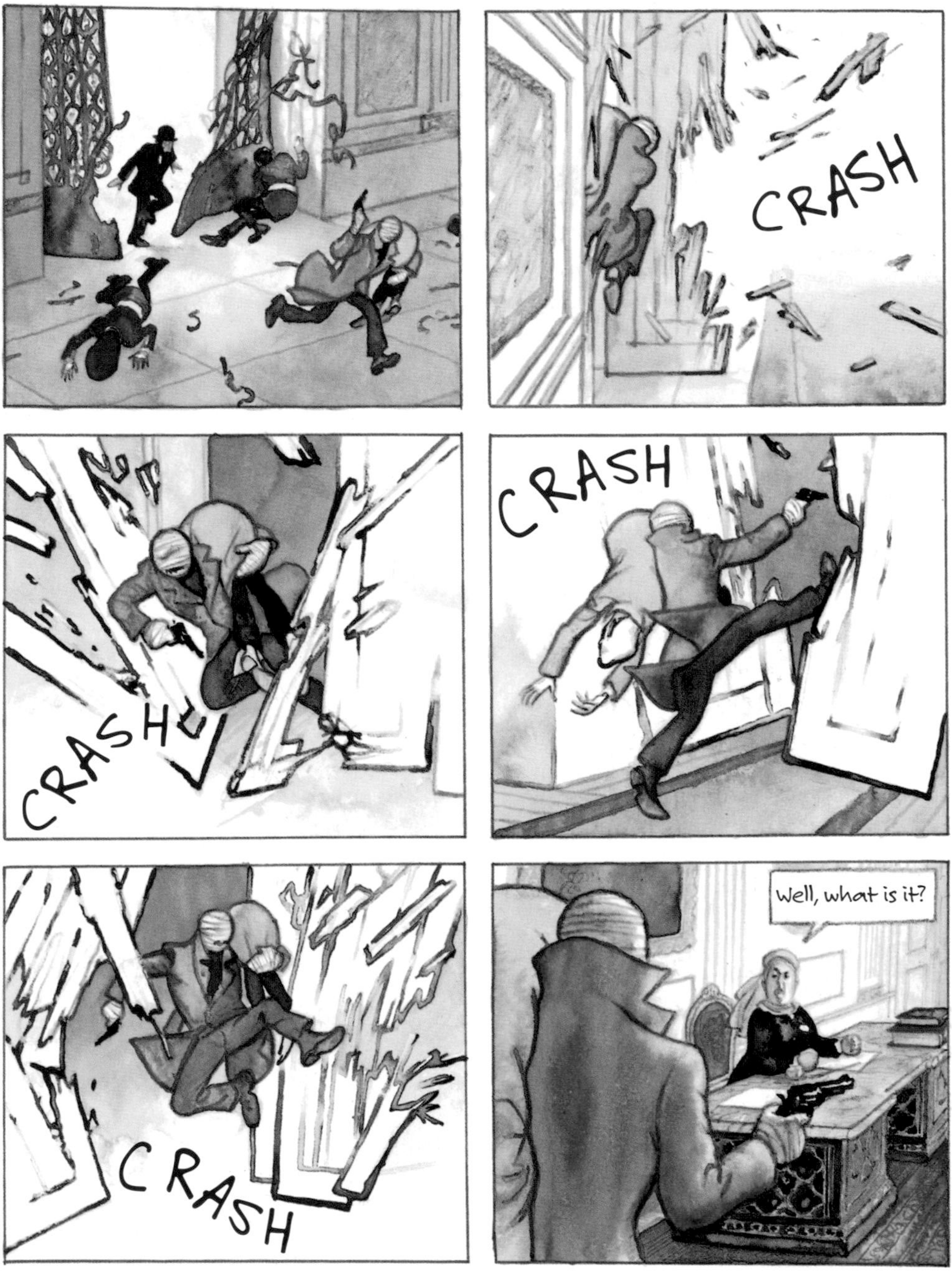
CRASH
CRASH
CRASH
CRASH
Well, what is it?

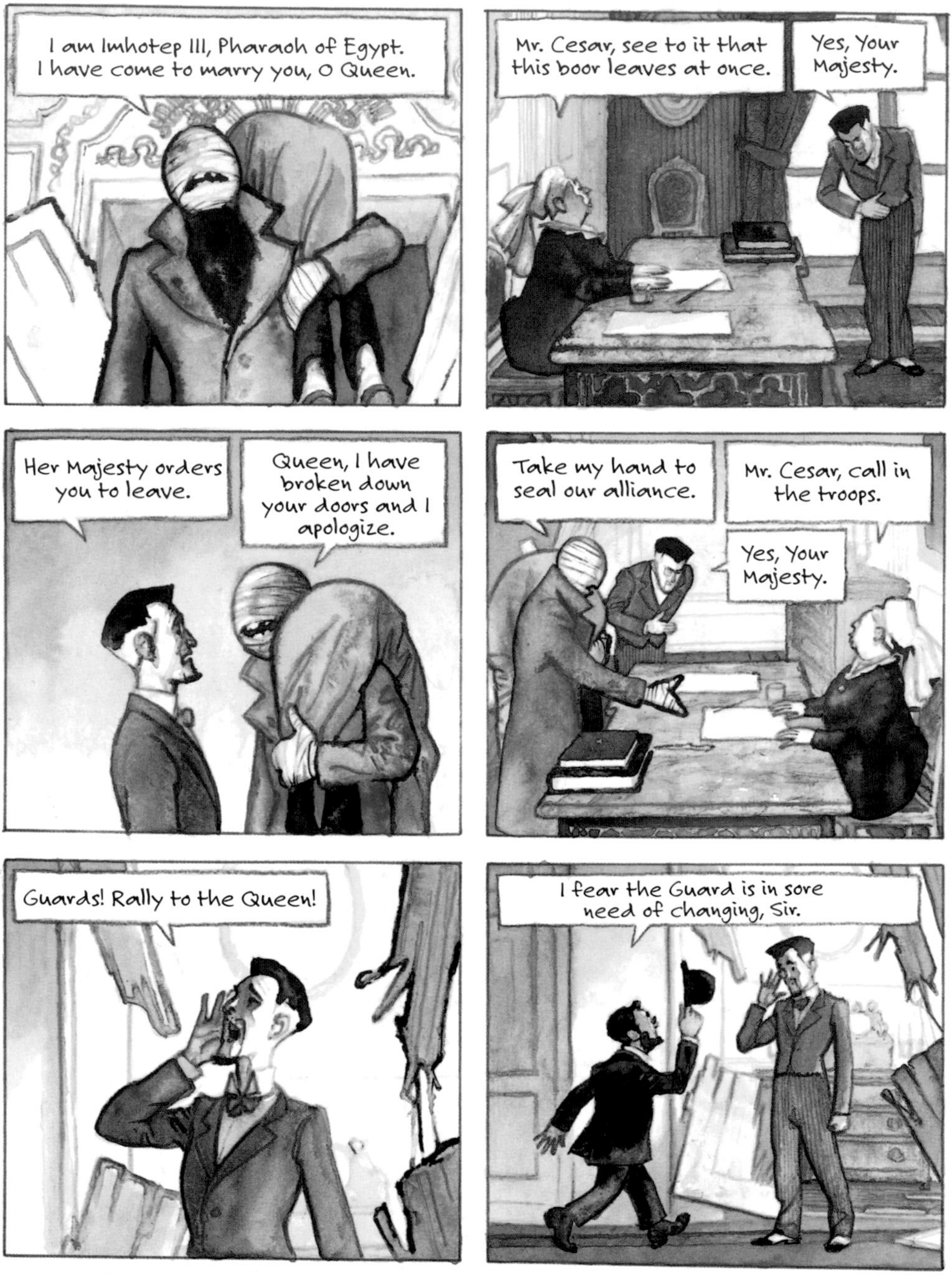
I am Imhotep III, Pharaoh of Egypt. I have come to marry you, O Queen.
Mr. Cesar, see to it that this boor leaves at once.
Yes, Your Majesty.
Her Majesty orders you to leave.
Queen, I have broken down your doors and I apologize.
Take my hand to seal our alliance.
Mr. Cesar, call in the troops.
Yes, Your Majesty.
Guards! Rally to the Queen!
I fear the Guard is in sore need of changing, Sir.

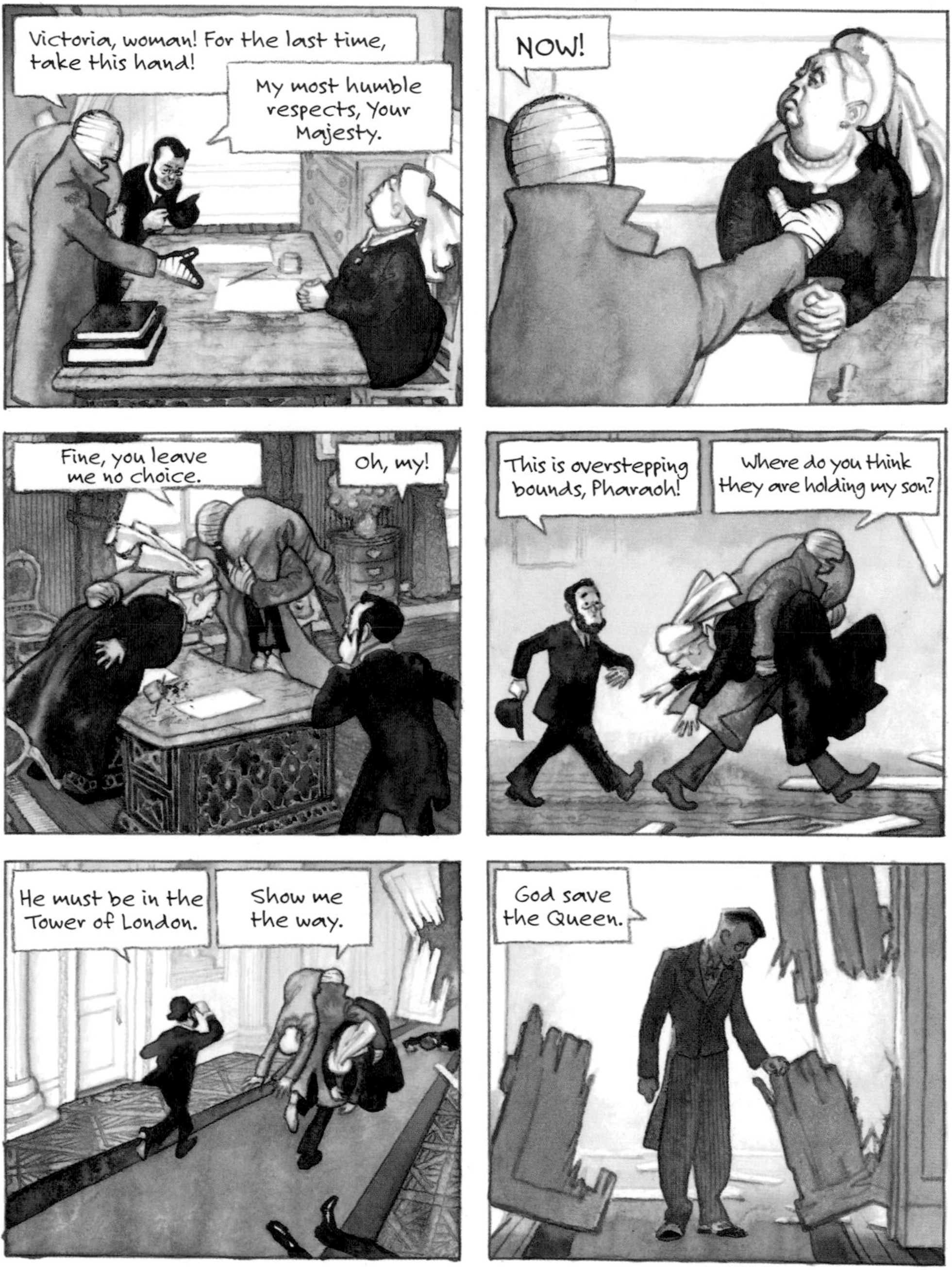
Victoria, woman! For the last time, take this hand!
My most humble respects, Your Majesty.
NOW!
Fine, you leave me no choice.
Oh, my!
This is overstepping bounds, Pharaoh!
Where do you think they are holding my son?
He must be in the Tower of London.
Show me the way.
God save the Queen.

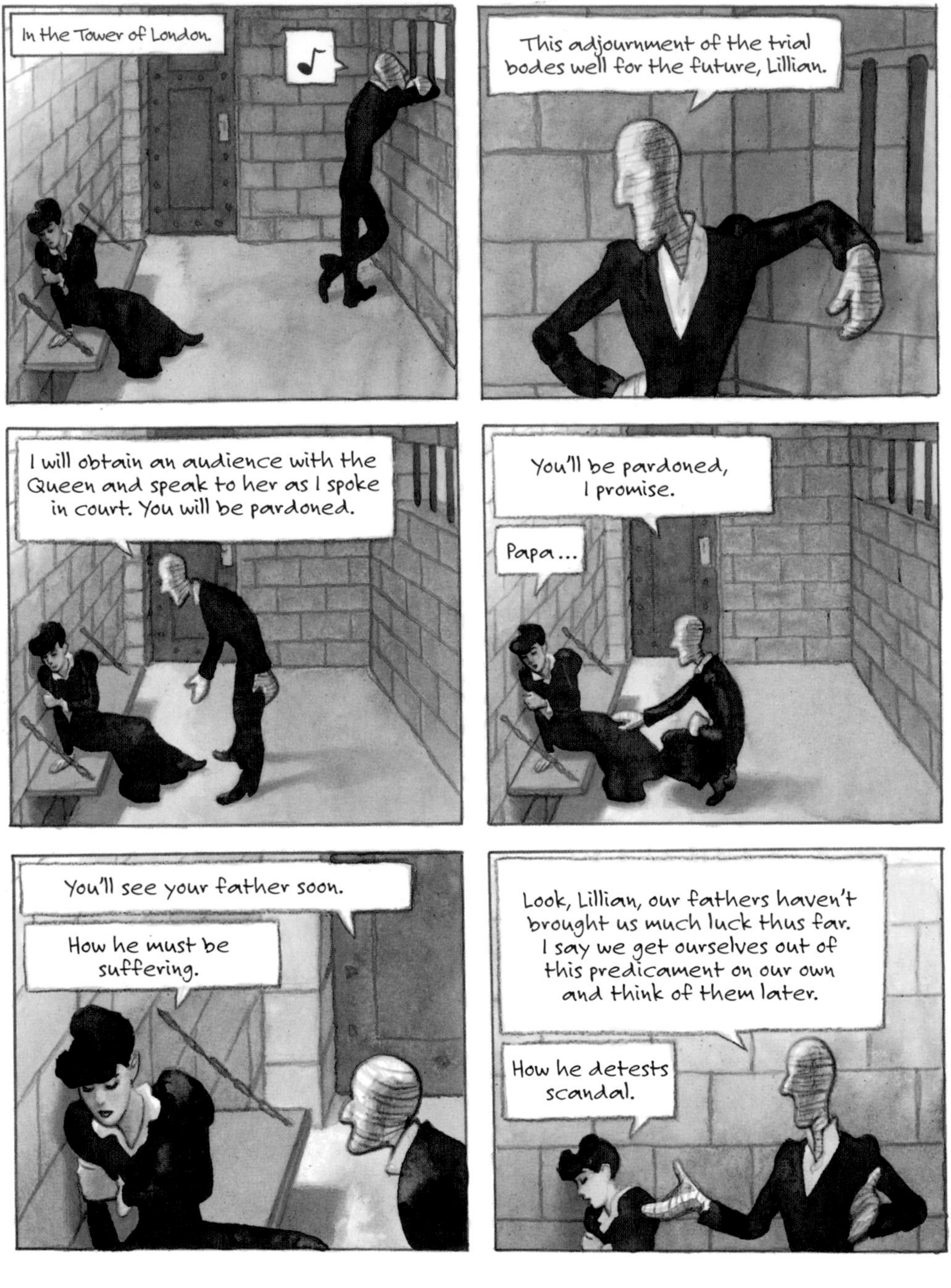
In the Tower of London.
♪
This adjournment of the trial bodes well for the future, Lillian.
I will obtain an audience with the Queen and speak to her as I spoke in court. You will be pardoned.
You'll be pardoned, I promise.
Papa...
You'll see your father soon.
How he must be suffering.
Look, Lillian, our fathers haven't brought us much luck thus far. I say we get ourselves out of this predicament on our own and think of them later.
How he detests scandal.

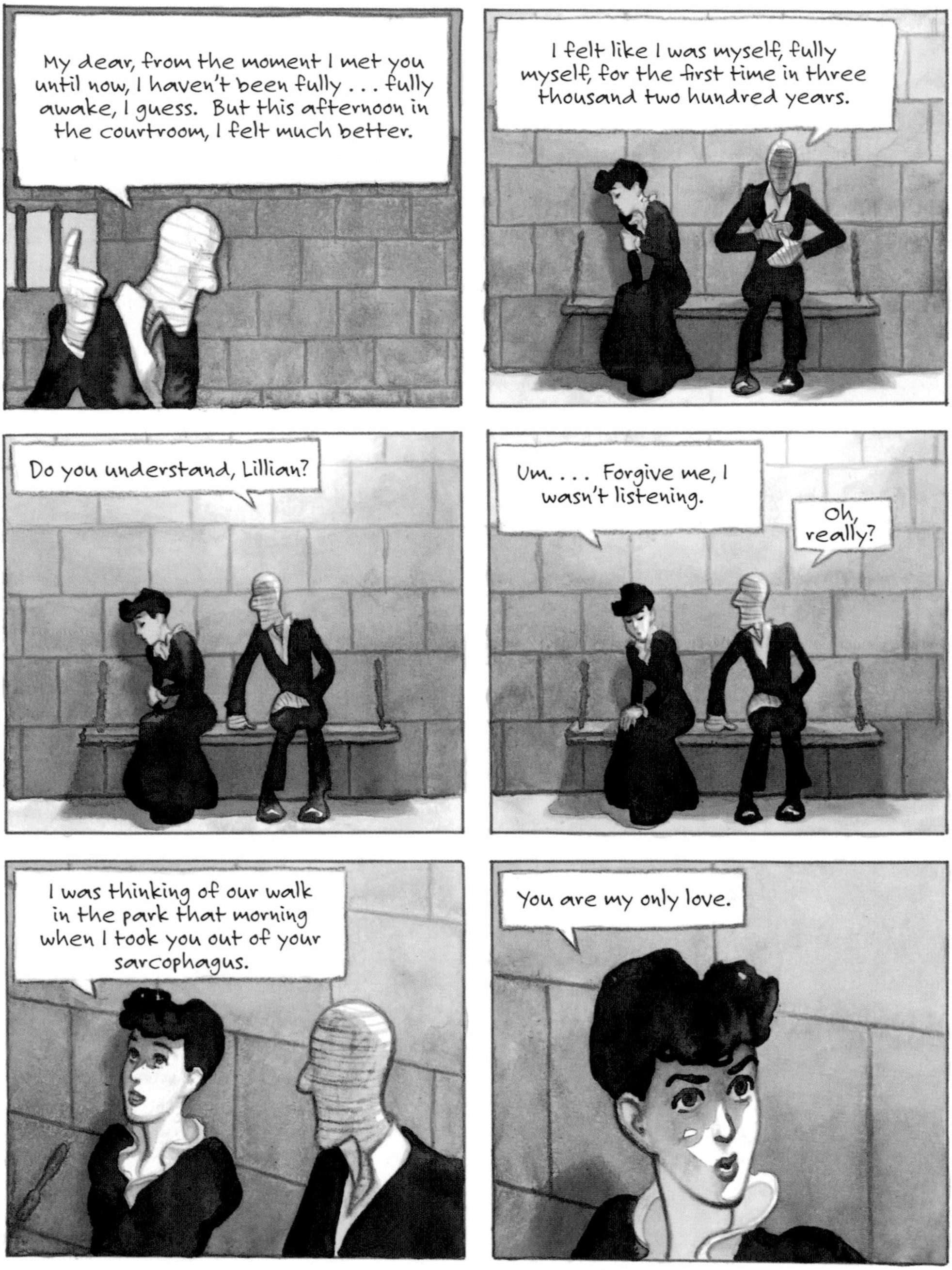
My dear, from the moment I met you until now, I haven't been fully . . . fully awake, I guess. But this afternoon in the courtroom, I felt much better.
I felt like I was myself, fully myself, for the first time in three thousand two hundred years.
Do you understand, Lillian?
Um. . . . Forgive me, I wasn't listening.
Oh, really?
I was thinking of our walk in the park that morning when I took you out of your sarcophagus.
You are my only love.

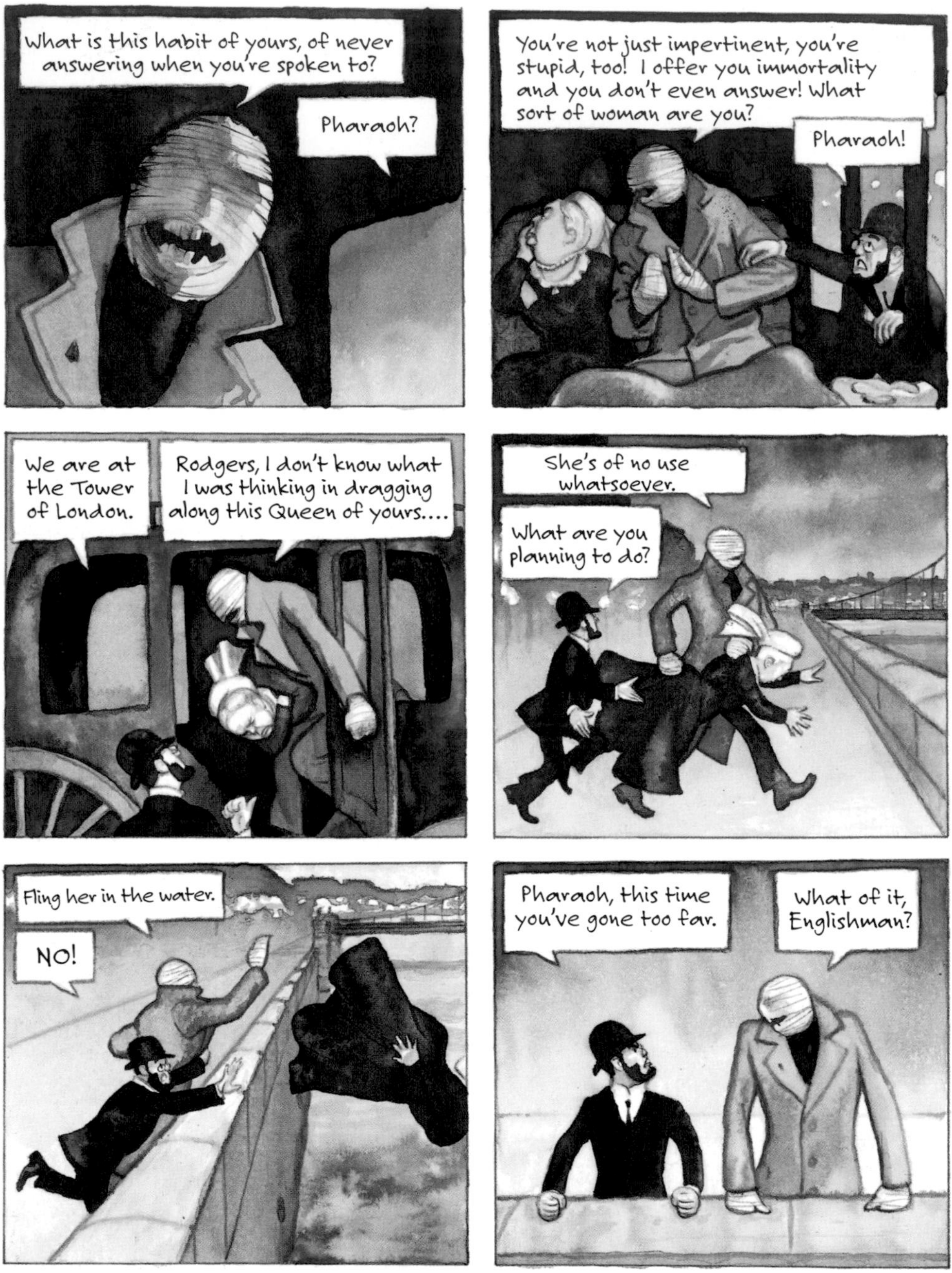

What is this habit of yours, of never answering when you're spoken to?
Pharaoh?
You're not just impertinent, you're stupid, too! I offer you immortality and you don't even answer! What sort of woman are you?
Pharaoh!
We are at the Tower of London.
Rodgers, I don't know what I was thinking in dragging along this Queen of yours....
She's of no use whatsoever.
What are you planning to do?
Fling her in the water.
NO!
Pharaoh, this time you've gone too far.
What of it, Englishman?

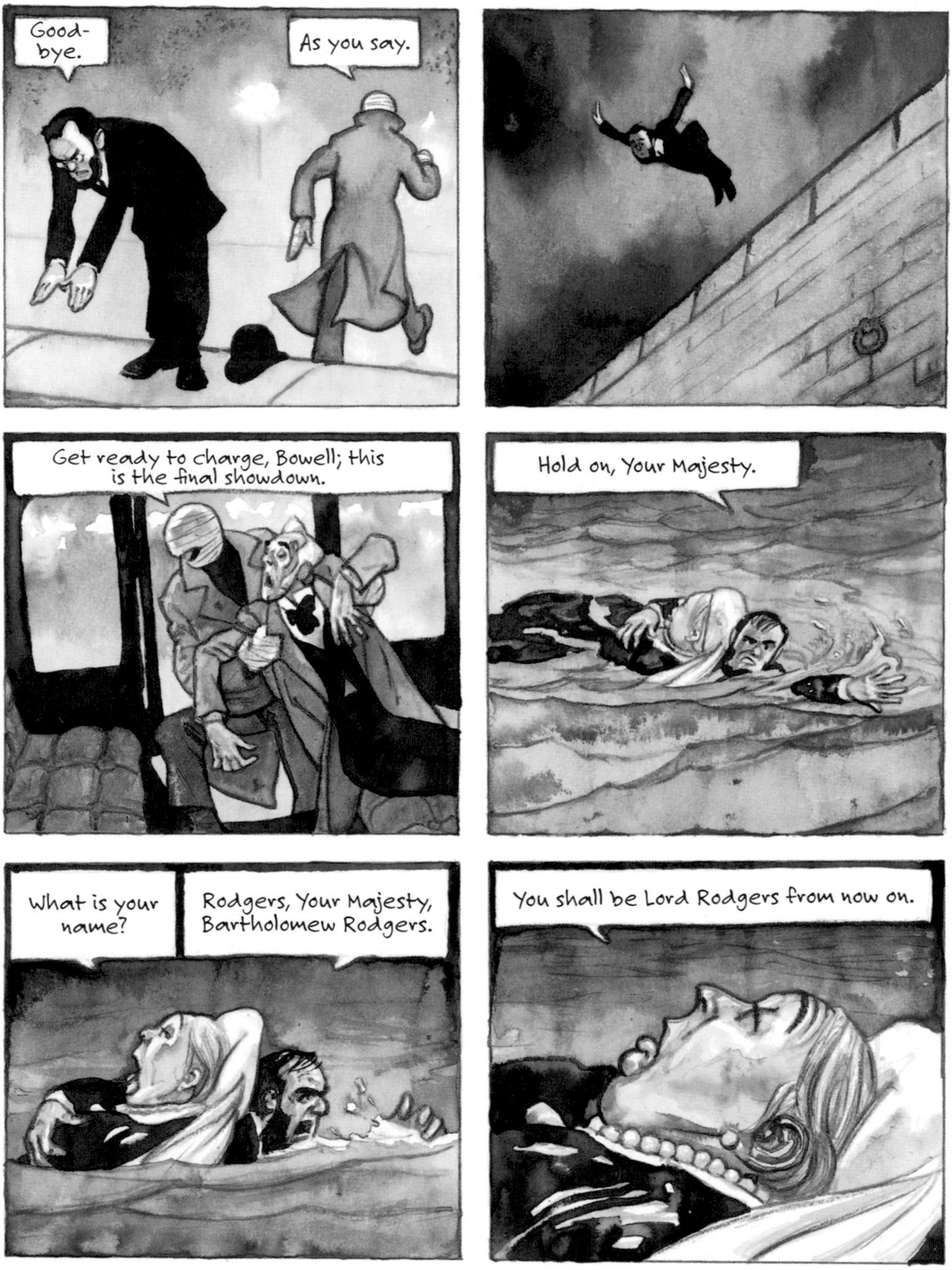
Good-bye.
As you say.
Get ready to charge, Bowell; this is the final showdown.
Hold on, Your Majesty.
What is your name?
Rodgers, Your Majesty, Bartholomew Rodgers.
You shall be Lord Rodgers from now on.

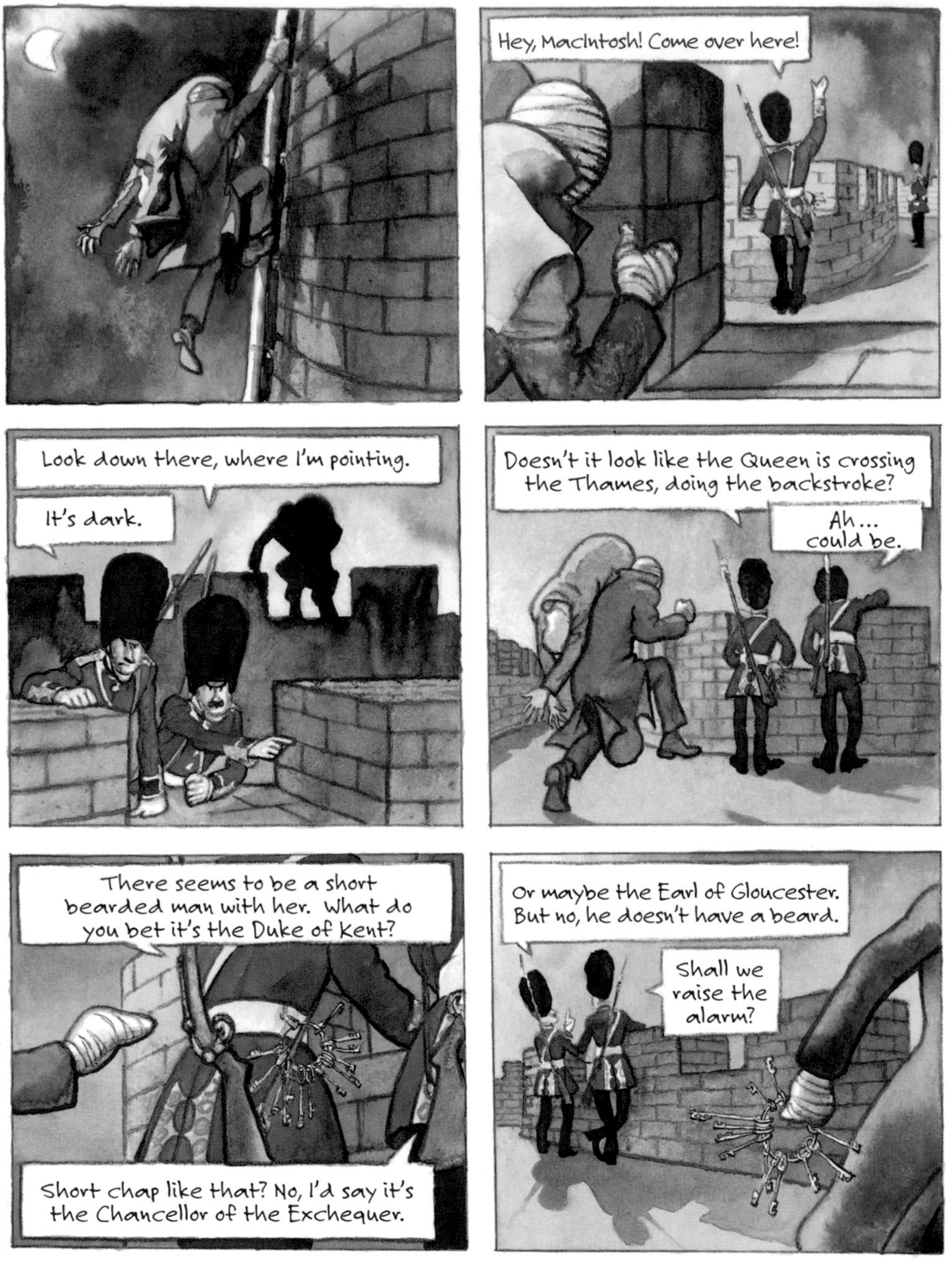
Hey, MacIntosh! Come over here!
Look down there, where I'm pointing.
It's dark.
Doesn't it look like the Queen is crossing the Thames, doing the backstroke?
Ah... could be.
There seems to be a short bearded man with her. What do you bet it's the Duke of Kent?
Short chap like that? No, I'd say it's the Chancellor of the Exchequer.
Or maybe the Earl of Gloucester. But no, he doesn't have a beard.
Shall we raise the alarm?

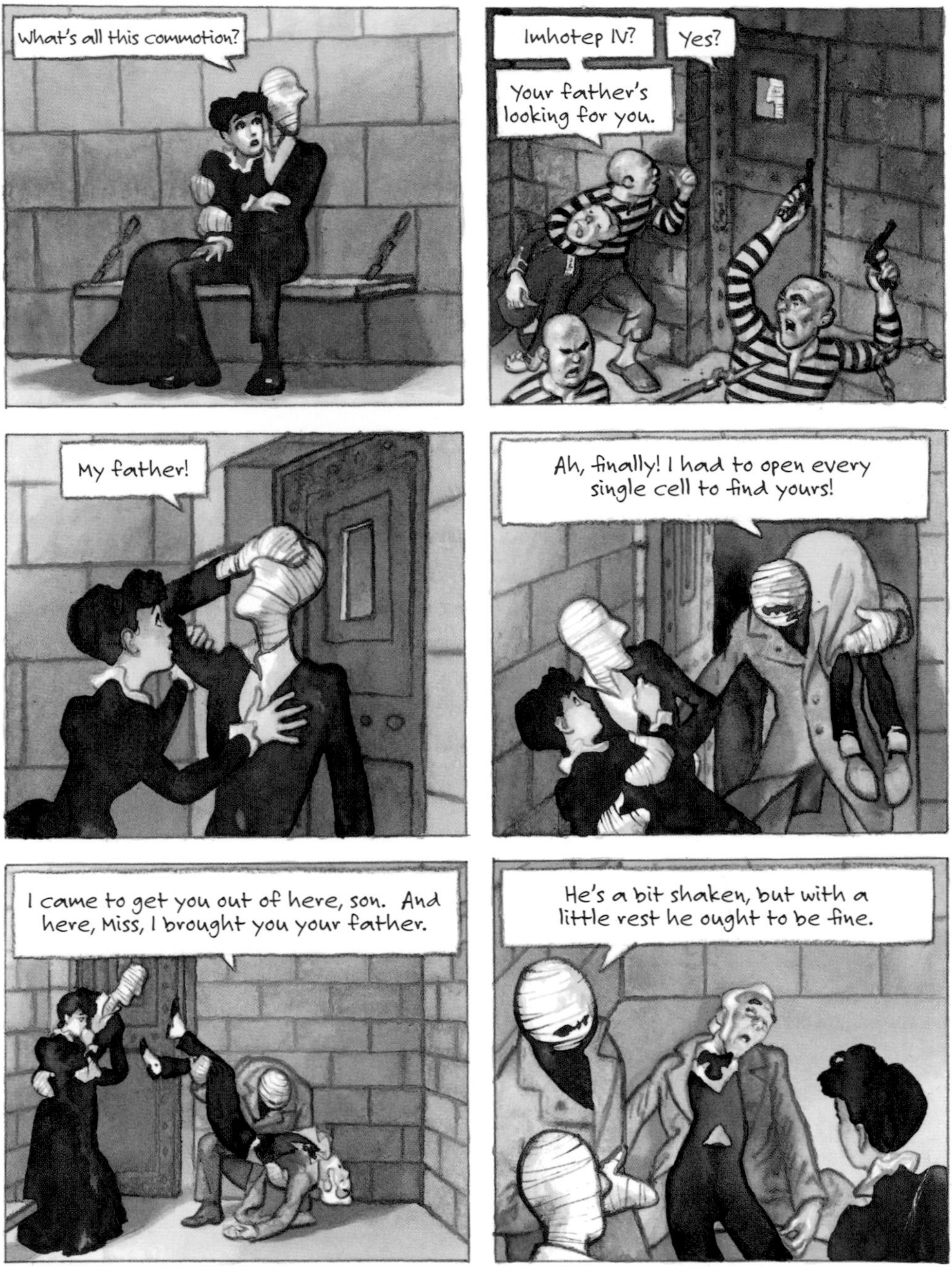
What's all this commotion?
Imhotep IV?
Yes?
Your father's looking for you.
My father!
Ah, finally! I had to open every single cell to find yours!
I came to get you out of here, son. And here, Miss, I brought you your father.
He's a bit shaken, but with a little rest he ought to be fine.

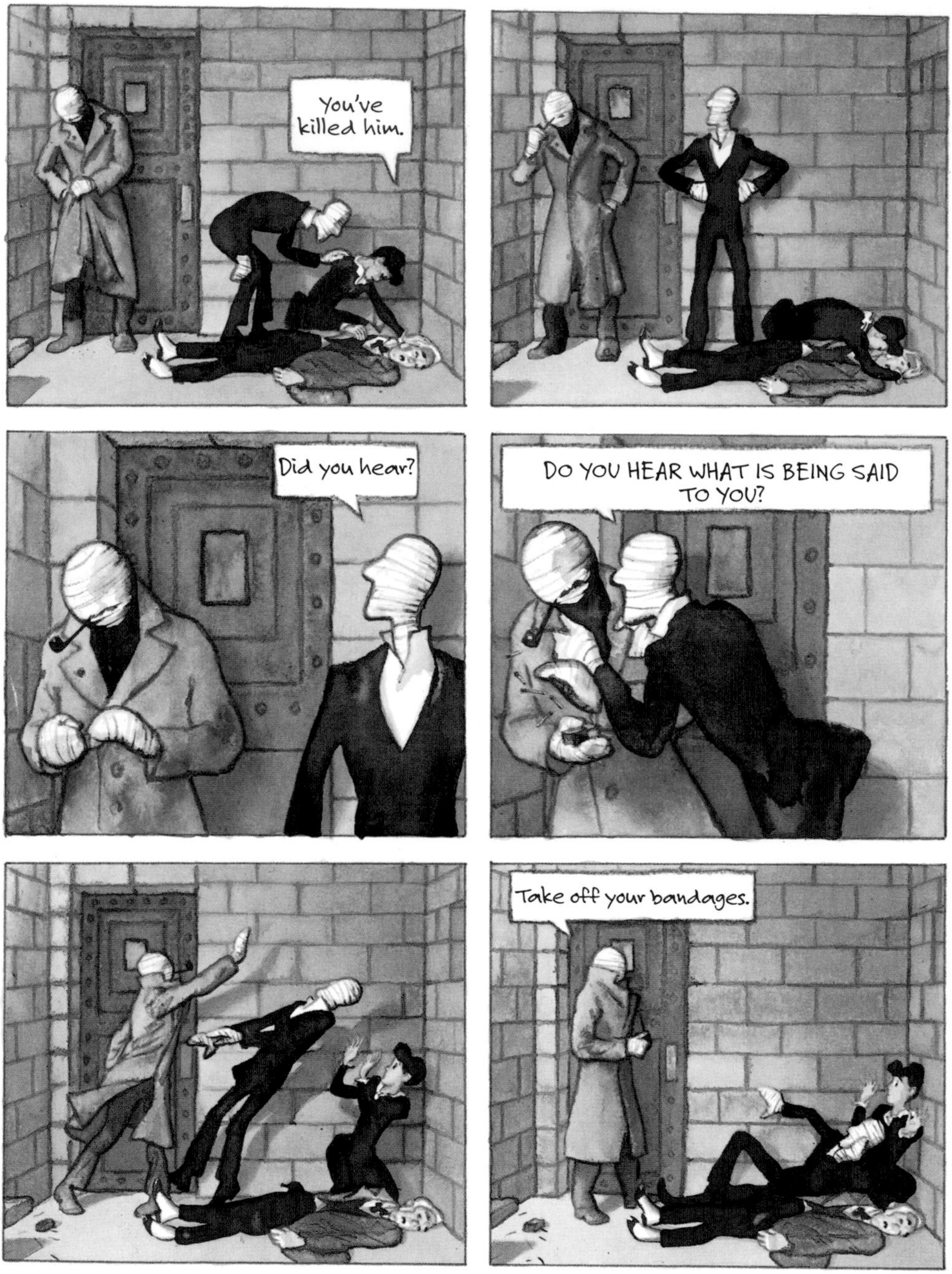
You've killed him.
Did you hear?
DO YOU HEAR WHAT IS BEING SAID TO YOU?
Take off your bandages.

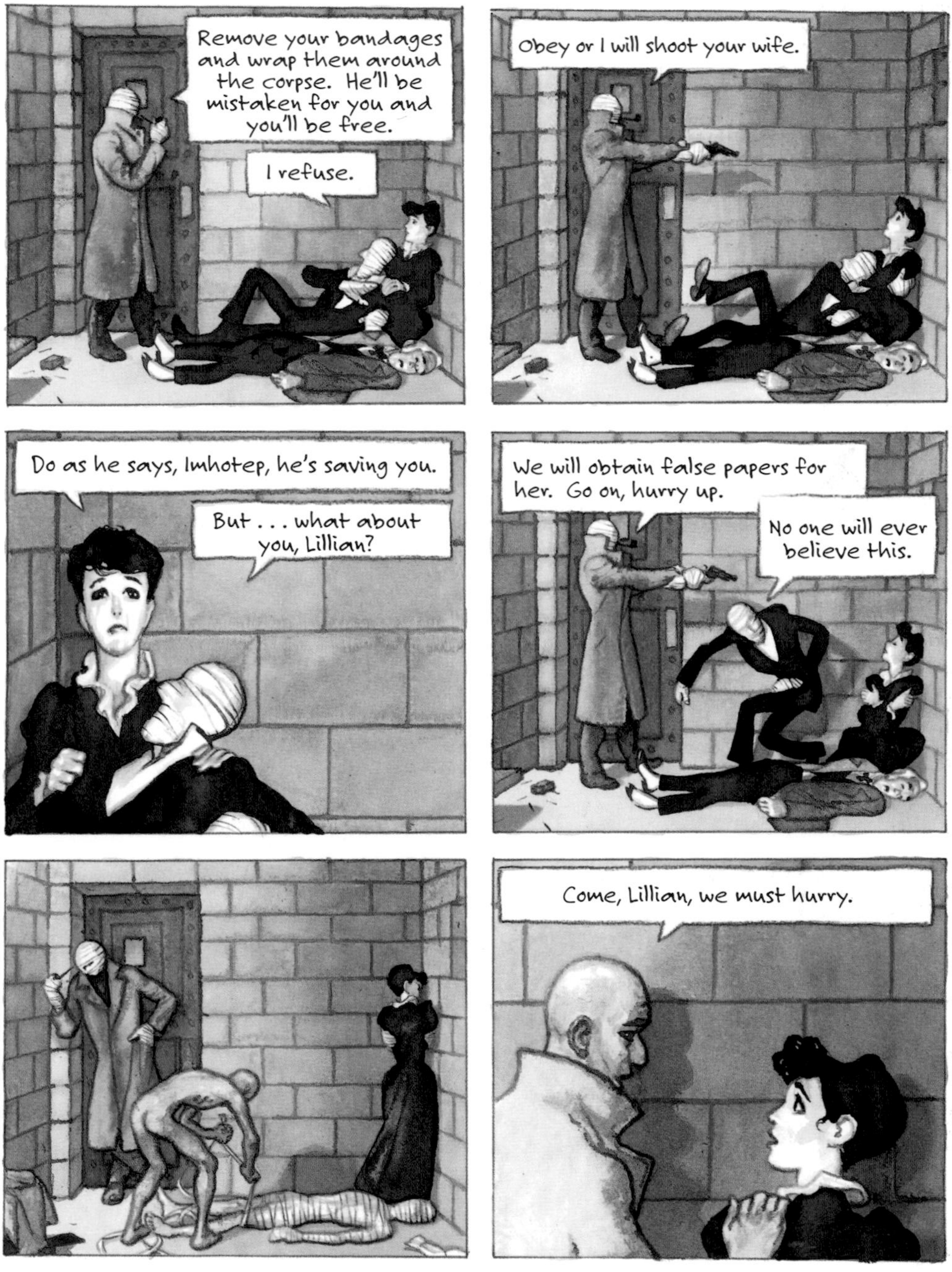
Remove your bandages and wrap them around the corpse. He'll be mistaken for you and you'll be free.
I refuse.
Obey or I will shoot your wife.
Do as he says, Imhotep, he's saving you.
But . . . what about you, Lillian?
We will obtain false papers for her. Go on, hurry up.
No one will ever believe this.
Come, Lillian, we must hurry.

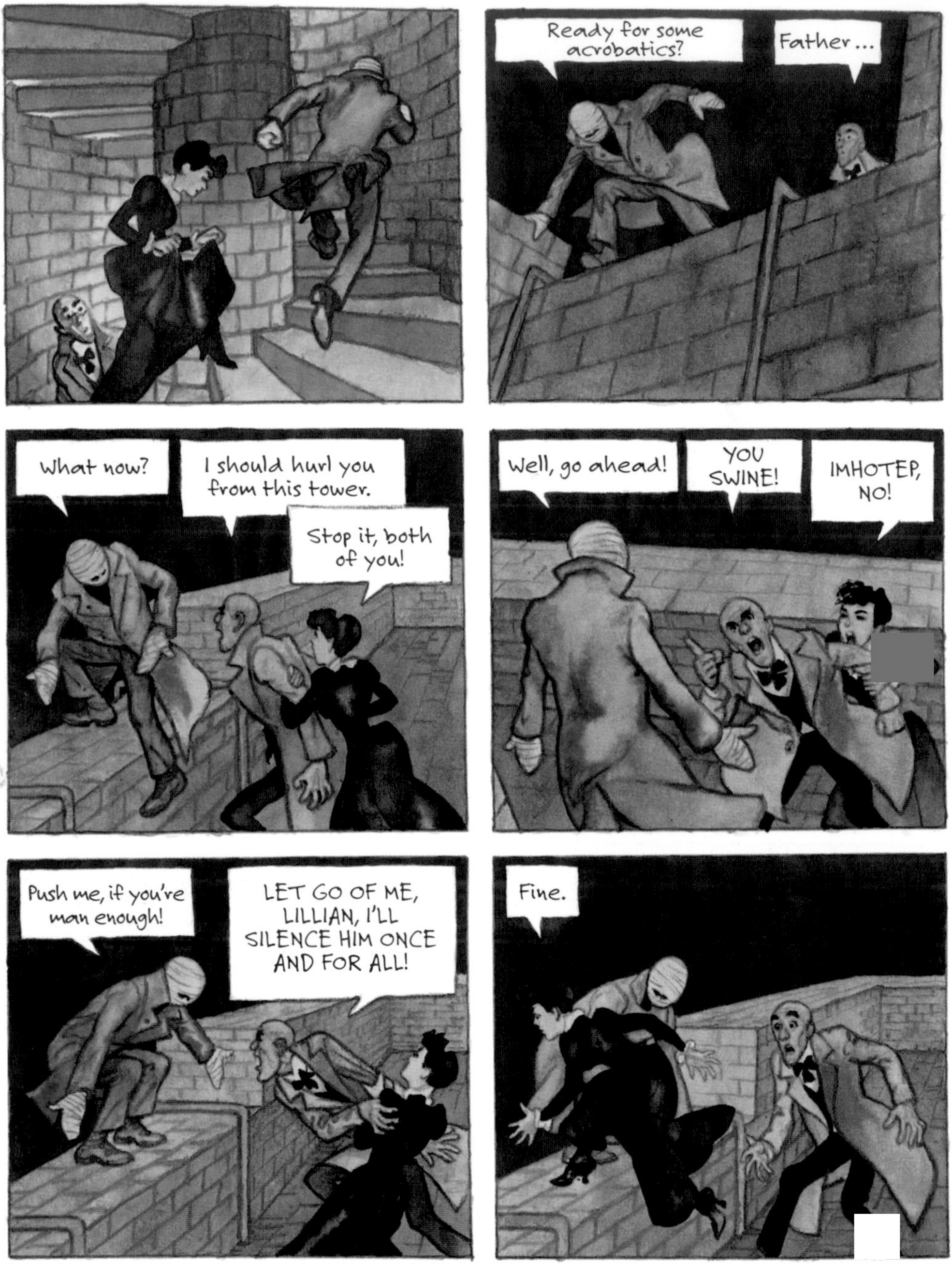

Ready for some acrobatics?
Father...
What now?
I should hurl you from this tower.
Stop it, both of you!
Well, go ahead!
YOU SWINE!
IMHOTEP, NO!
Push me, if you're man enough!
LET GO OF ME, LILLIAN, I'LL SILENCE HIM ONCE AND FOR ALL!
Fine.

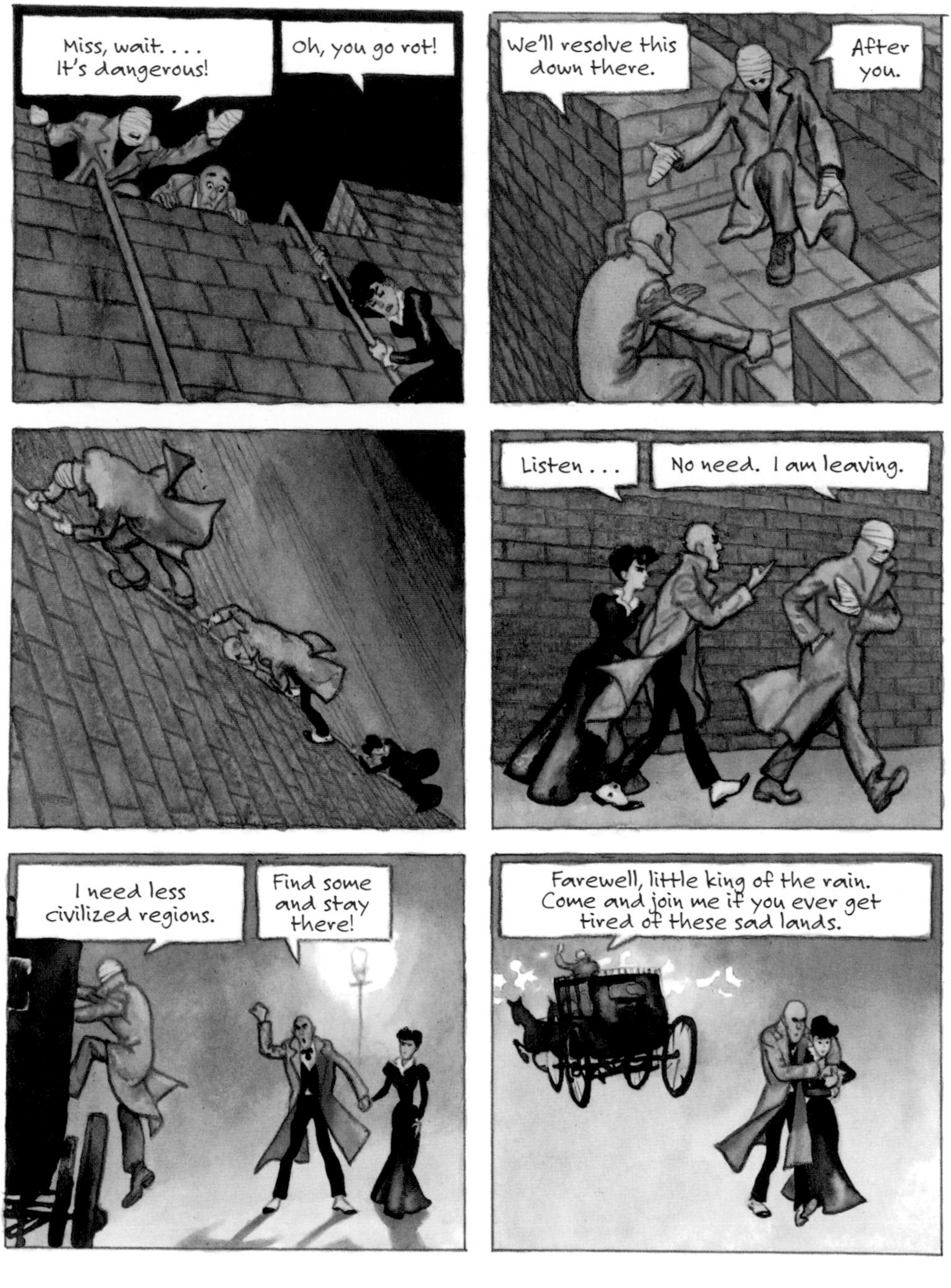
Miss, wait. . . .
It's dangerous!
Oh, you go rot!
We'll resolve this down there.
After you.
Listen . . .
No need. I am leaving.
I need less civilized regions.
Find some and stay there!
Farewell, little king of the rain. Come and join me if you ever get tired of these sad lands.

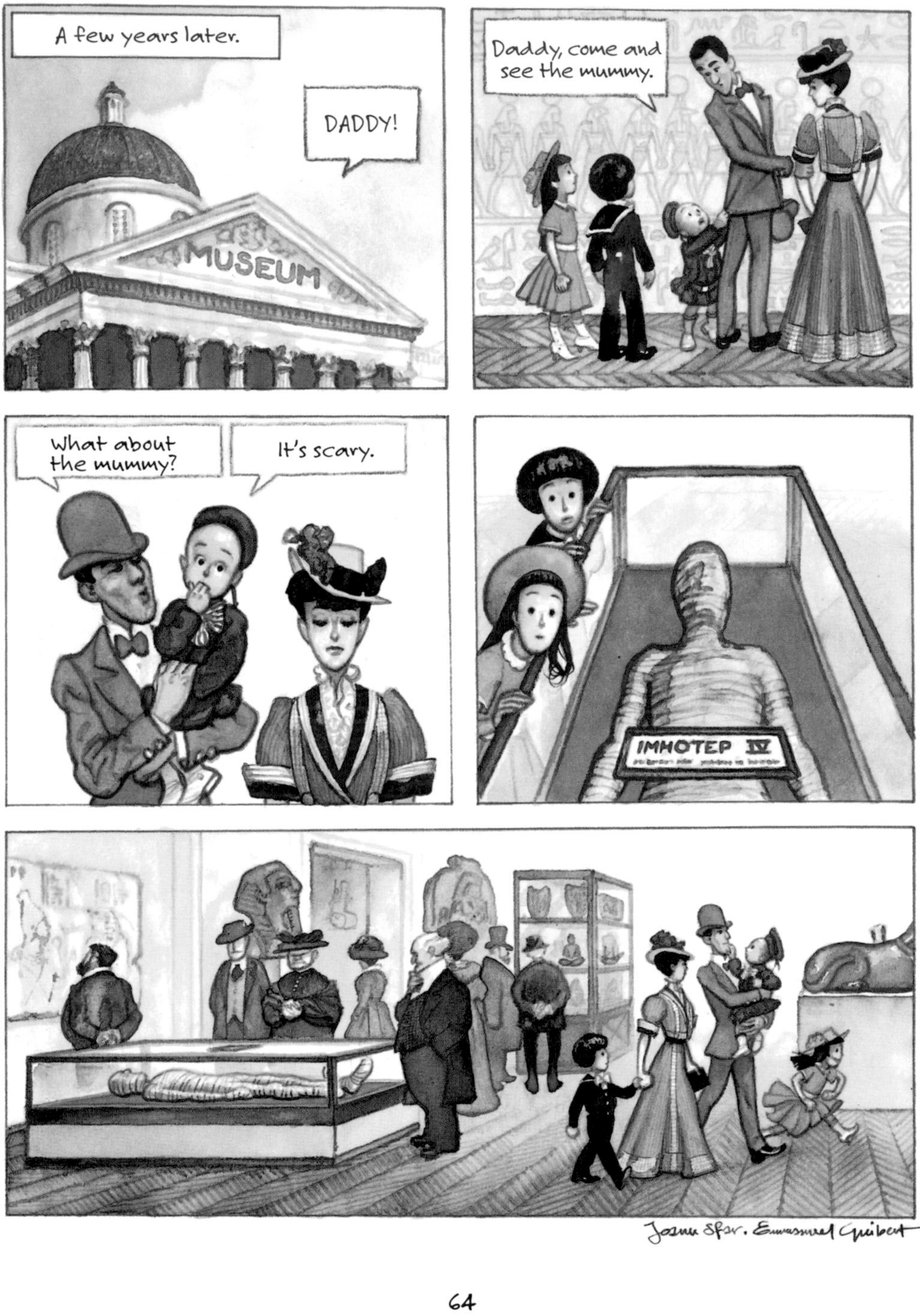
A few years later.
DADDY!
MUSEUM
Daddy, come and see the mummy.
What about the mummy?
It's scary.
IMHOTEP IV
Joann Sfar. Emmanuel Guibert

London Sketches

FROM THE BRITISH MUSEUM AND
THE STREETS OF LONDON, 1997

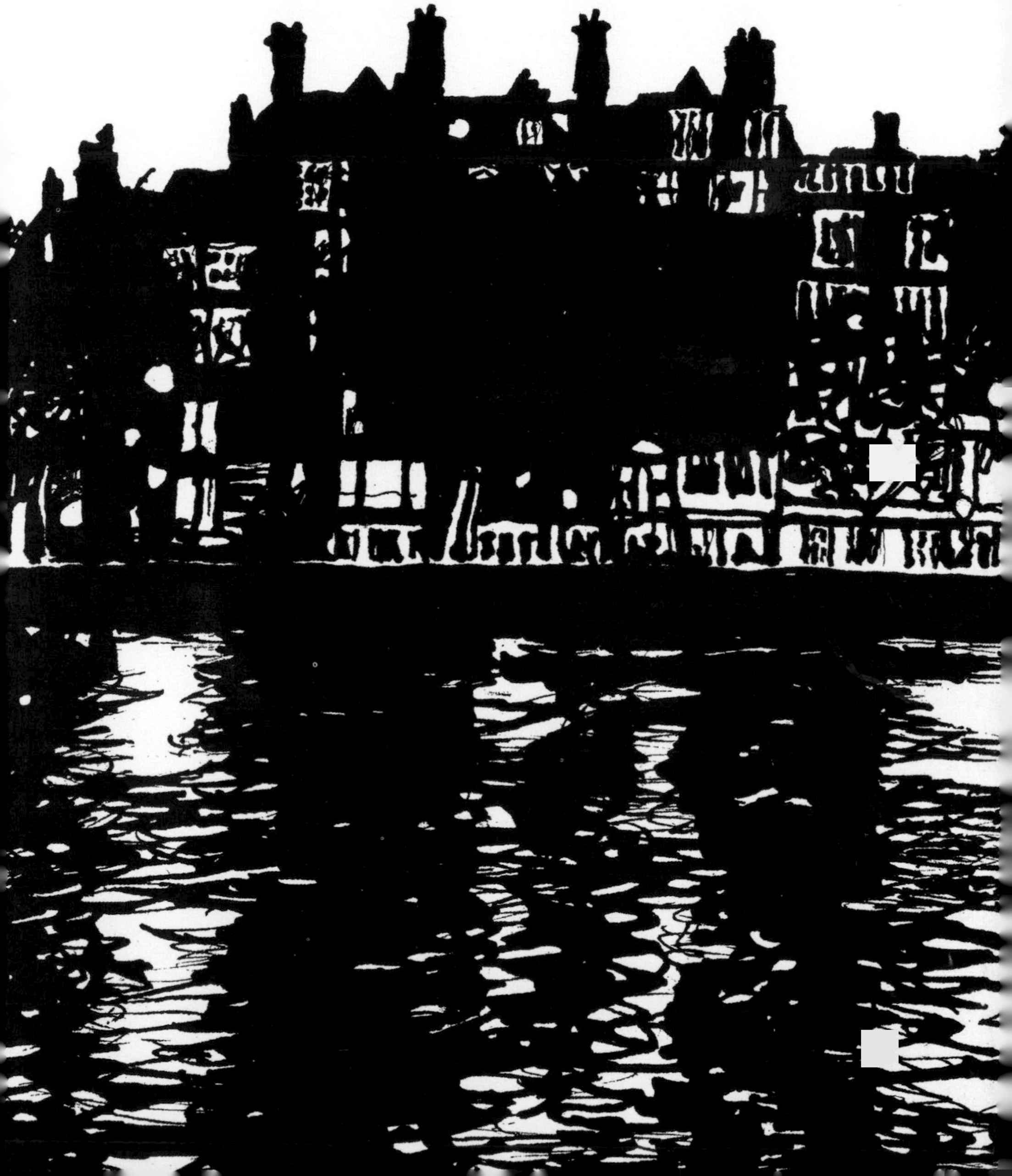

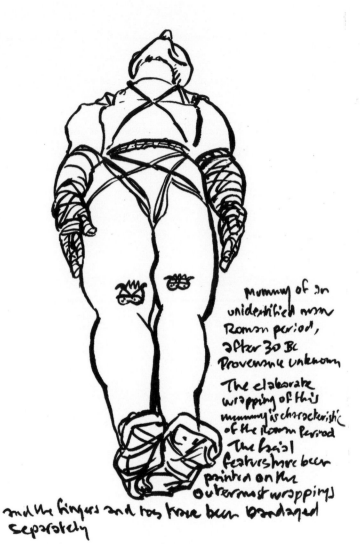

mummy of an
unidentified man
Roman period,
after 30 BC
Provenance unknown

The elaborate
wrapping of this
mummy is characteristic
of the Roman period
The facial
features have been
painted on the
outermost wrappings
and the fingers and toes have been bandaged
separately

Naturally preserved body
of a man in a reconstructed
grave-pit, with a selection of
typical grave goods.
Late predynastic, Nagada II
About 3400 BC

The sarcophagus of SETI I
King of Egypt in about
1370 B.C., is formed out
of a single block of semi
-transparent limestone.
The sarcophagus, as well as
its cover (of which fragments
are preserved in the museum)
are incised, inside and out,
with scenes and texts from
a religious book called the
BOOK OF THE GATES. This
was compiled with a view
to instructing the Egyptian
worshipper of Osiris and Ra
in the nature of the regions
through which his soul would
pass after death and the
character of the beings whom
he would meet there; in short
it was intended as a guide to
the underworld. On the
bottom of the sarcophagus
is a figure of the goddess
NUT, to whose keeping
the body of the dead being
was committed.

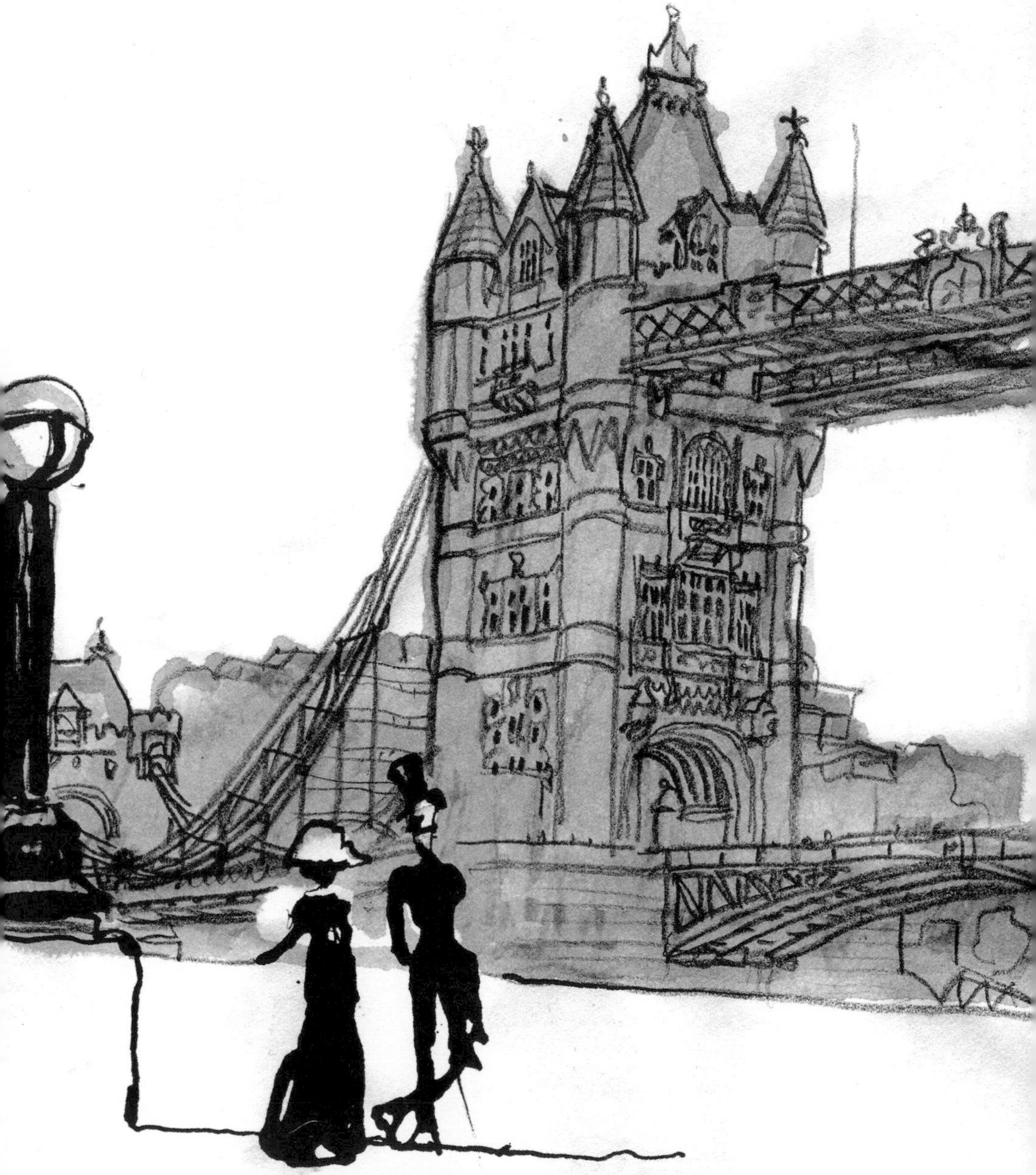

57 Albert Bridge Road

Thomas
Carlyle

First Second

New York & London

Copyright © 1997 by
Emmanuel Guibert and Joann Sfar
English translation copyright © 2007 by
First Second

Published by First Second
First Second is an imprint of Roaring Brook Press,
a division of Holtzbrinck Publishing Holdings Limited Partnership
175 Fifth Avenue, New York, NY 10010

Distributed in Canada by H. B. Fenn and Company Ltd.
Distributed in the United Kingdom by Macmillan Children's Books, a division of Pan
Macmillan.

Originally published in France in 1997 under the title *La fille du professeur* by Editions
Dupuis, Paris.

Design by Danica Novgorodoff

Library of Congress Cataloging-in-Publication Data

Guibert, Emmanuel.
[Fille du professeur. English]
The professor's daughter / illustrated by Emmanuel Guibert ; story
by Joann Sfar ; translated by Alexis Siegel. -- 1st American ed.
p. cm.
ISBN-13: 978-1-59643-130-0 (paperback)
ISBN-10: 1-59643-130-X (paperback)

COLLECTOR'S EDITION
ISBN-13: 978-1-59643-255-0
ISBN-10: 1-59643-255-1

1. Graphic novels.   I. Sfar, Joann. II. Title.
PN6747.G85F5613 2007
741.5'944--dc22

2006022177

First Second books are available for special promotions and premiums.
For details, contact: Director of Special Markets, Holtzbrinck Publishers.

First American Edition May 2007

Printed in China

10 9 8 7 6 5 4 3 2 1